I0202790

Using
Oral History
in Community
History Projects

Laurie Mercier
Madeline Buckendorf

ORAL HISTORY
ASSOCIATION

About the Authors　　Laurie Mercier is Associate Professor of History at Washington State University Vancouver and author of *Anaconda: Labor, Community, and Culture in Montana's Smelter City* (University of Illinois), and *Mining Women: Gender in the Development of a Global Industry* (Palgrave/McMillan). Mercier holds a Ph.D. in History from the University of Oregon (1995), is a former president of the Oral History Association (1999–2000), and former Montana Historical Society oral historian (1981–1988).

Madeline Kelley Buckendorf has worked for more than twenty-five years in the field of public history. She has directed community, history, and cultural resource projects in Idaho, Oregon, Washington, and Nevada, and directed the Idaho Oral History Center for the Idaho State Historical Society from 1978 to 1989. Buckendorf serves as a consulting historian to federal, state, local, and private agencies and organizations. She received her B.A. in English Literature from The College of Idaho (now Albertson College of Idaho) in 1974, and her Master's Degree in Public History from Boise State University in 1993.

About the Oral History Association　　The Oral History Association is a society of scholars, students, local historians, and others concerned with the application of professional standards to the collection, preservation, dissemination, and use of oral testimony. It serves as a bridge between scholars of various disciplines and also between these scholars and librarians, archivists, teachers, journalists, authors, and others engaged in recording personal and institutional histories. Members of the Oral History Association exchange views and learn of new developments through the annual meeting, a newsletter published three times a year, the *Oral History Review,* and this pamphlet series. Pamphlets offer basic and useful information about many aspects of conducting, interpreting, processing, and publishing oral history interviews and managing oral history programs and projects. For more information about membership in the Oral History Association and to order copies of other pamphlets in the series, please contact the Oral History Association at Dickinson College, P. O. Box 1773, Carlisle, PA 17013-2396; oha@dickinson.edu, http://www.dickinson.edu/oha.

©2007 by the Oral History Association. All rights reserved.

Printed in the United States of America

We are grateful to the following Oral History Association members for their generous assistance in this pamphlet revision: editor Irene Reti, John Wolford, Teresa Bergen, Kathy Nasstrom, Madelyn Campbell, Donna Sinclair, and Rose Diaz. Thanks are due, too, to the many community history project directors who shared information, listed in Section 3, and to Barbara Allen Bogart and Jessie Embry for their guidance on the original 1992 pamphlet. Kristin Driscoll designed and produced the pamphlet.

All human beings are practicing historians. As we go through life we present ourselves to others through our life story; as we grow and mature we change that story through different inter-pretations and different emphasis. We stress different events as having been decisive at different times in our life history and, as we do so, we give those events new meanings. People do not think of this as "doing history"; they engage in it often without special awareness. We live our lives; we tell our stories. It is as natural as breathing.

Gerda Lerner, *Why History Matters: Life and Thought*

CONTENTS

An interest in the past often begins with history that is close at hand. We may come across an old photograph of our hometown and wonder what happened to the old buildings. We may notice that the city in which we live contains a number of distinctive ethnic neighborhoods and become curious about their origins. We may meet an older resident of our community and become fascinated with her memories of the events of fifty years ago. When we develop an interest in and questions about the local past, we can undertake a community history project to learn more. Such projects often begin with collections of newspapers, letters, memoirs, diaries, artifacts, and photographs. These materials are often the most tangible and accessible sources of information about the local past. But there is another valuable kind of historical resource that we may overlook: personal memories of the community's history.

Since the 1970s, the use of oral history in community history projects has increased markedly. Many such projects have been successful, but many others have been launched with great enthusiasm, only to languish, die, or produce uneven results. These failures are often the result of inadequate planning or unskilled execution rather than the fault of the oral history method itself. This pamphlet is designed to guide individuals and groups who wish to use oral history in community history projects. It contains specific suggestions on setting up and carrying out such projects and addresses common concerns.

What is a Community?

The term community encompasses nearly every kind of human group conceivable, from a family to political, cultural, occupational, or religious organizations whose membership is far-flung. Whatever its size or constituency, a community consists of individuals bound together by a sense of shared identity. Often that identity is grounded in past experiences, in a shared history. Those experiences can stem from living in the same place, doing the same kind of work, or simply possessing a common background or national origin. Whatever its basis, that sense of a shared past is what community history projects explore.

Community History and Oral History

To undertake a community history project is to engage in the oldest form of historical research. Through the centuries, indigenous people, migrants to new places, and chroniclers preserved and passed on or wrote about their memories of communities. Even when history as a field became professionalized in the nineteenth century and its scope broadened, the tradition of community history continued, largely in the hands of self-taught local historians. The work of these individuals has tended to rely primarily on written records and even material artifacts. But not all the aspects of a community's past are represented in these sources. The memories of individual members of the community contain a wealth of information, information that is usually not available in any other form. Oral history taps these memories and, used in conjunction with other historical resources, creates a richer picture of a community's history. It is an invaluable means of incorporating everyday experience into the historical record. By giving voice to people excluded or ignored in the usual historical sources, oral history can provide a fuller, more honest picture of the past by answering the hows and whys of human actions, by fleshing out the bare bones of raw statistics and official reports, and by dealing with sobering as well as positive experiences. Perhaps most importantly, it can involve community members in the process of defining what is important about their own past.

The initial impetus for doing community history is often curiosity and a desire to preserve one's past. But community historical research has other values as well. It enables individuals to see their personal experiences and the community's history within the context of the larger regional, national, and global contexts. In practice, community history projects that go beyond the written documentary sources to record the personal recollections of a cross-section of community members can significantly expand community members' understanding of their identity, their history, and their connection with other communities. If an oral history component of a community history project is carefully planned and well researched, it can produce a more accurate picture of the complexity and diversity of a community's heritage. It could also potentially contribute to a broader understanding of American history and culture.

How This Pamphlet Is Organized

Because good preparation is the key to a successful community oral history project, we provide a detailed, step-by-step guide to project planning and execution in Section 1. There are many other publications, some of which are featured at the end of the pamphlet, that elaborate interview techniques, the recording and preservation of interviews, and the uses of oral history. Our emphasis here is on planning and implementing community projects. In Section 2 we address common pitfalls that may arise in an oral history project and suggest ways to avoid or minimize them. Section 3 features sample projects from across the country that in the last decade successfully used oral history in creative and meaningful ways to illuminate community history. Finally, we include some suggested resources to direct readers to more specific guidance about oral history methods and means of interpretation.

Much has happened in the world of oral history since this pamphlet was originally published in 1992. Most dramatic is the change in technology, both in terms of recording—from analog to digital—and in preserving and presenting interviews through the World Wide Web. The fact that demand for this Oral History Association pamphlet remained high, even when no longer in print, and that we found so many outstanding new community projects to profile, speaks to the continued popularity and growing sophistication of community oral history.

Get Started!

Crafting a project that will not stall or fail, that examines more than the surface of a community's history and its best-known personalities, and that will not disappear on a library shelf once the project is over requires organization and hard work. But it can also be fun and rewarding. The interviews you and your group create will instruct generations of community members and researchers. In this pamphlet, we describe how an oral history project can be set up and carried out as part of a community history project. For some projects, oral history will be the primary source of information; for other projects it will be used as part of a larger data-gathering effort. The practical suggestions we provide are applicable in both cases. They are intended to both help strengthen participant morale and the final outcome. We hope that those who are new to community oral history projects can learn from the experiences of others who have already struggled around (and sometimes through) the quicksand associated with these endeavors. The recommendations presented here are based on such experiences.

1

PLANNING, ORGANIZING, AND IMPLEMENTING
A COMMUNITY ORAL HISTORY PROJECT

Fired up with enthusiasm about oral history, many people begin recording reminiscences without first carefully thinking through the objectives of a project. While the planning stage of an oral history project lacks the glamor of asking people about their memories, the time it requires is essential for implementing a successful project and collecting valuable information that can contribute to the historical record. The planning process should involve community members in defining the purpose of the oral history project and setting goals. If goals are not set, the project is likely to produce a set of recordings that reveal very little, share no consistent theme, and consequently go unused. This section outlines the process of planning, organizing, and implementing a community oral history project. The following suggestions are intended to prevent frustrations and to promote quality interviews that enlighten both the community and a broader audience.

The Community Connection

By its very nature, community oral history relies on its own members to provide information, feedback, and support for every phase of a project. Community cooperation at every stage of the project is crucial, from mapping the project scope and aims, gaining access to privately-owned materials, gathering leads on information and names of people to interview, to disseminating the results of the project. Communities are also the beneficiaries of community oral history work. They are often the primary users of the oral sources and the chief audience for the project's final product. The final recordings and transcripts are made accessible to the community at a local repository or on the World Wide Web, and interpretive projects such as publications or media programs are of most interest to the community that was the project's focus.

The Planning or Advisory Committee

One of the first steps in developing a community oral history project is to create a planning committee that includes representatives from various segments of the community. An advisory committee for a study of a rural community undergoing rapid exurban growth, for example, might include long-time grain farmers, urban telecommuting transplants seeking rural solitude, and new organic truck farmers. A project on peace activists in the Pacific Northwest would seek grassroots, church, and veterans' representatives from a number of cities and towns in the region. From the community's diverse residents or members, select a committee who will provide a range of representative perspectives.

Practices in Oral History

Understanding the actual composition of a community is crucial for constructing a representative committee. In addition to well-known spokespersons such as the local historian, church ministers, librarians, and elected officials, seek out sectors of the community that may seem "hidden." You might discover, for example, that Mexican Americans comprise almost twenty percent of a community's population, but the local historical society and museum have not acknowledged their presence in publications or exhibits, and few of your community contacts have suggested any Latinos as potential committee members. Or a community may pride itself on its German-American heritage, as witnessed by an annual Oktoberfest, names of buildings, and school mascot. On further scrutiny, however, you may discover that Irish and Italian Americans were as numerous and as significant in the community's development. Or an ethnic group that appears homogeneous to outsiders may actually consist of differences based on economic class or periods of immigration. Diverse representation will help a community oral history project explore the complex nature of community life as all members have lived it.

An advisory committee composed of individuals representing a cross-section of the community needs to meet periodically to advise project organizers and guide the oral history process. The committee may suggest names of prospective interviewees, assist with introductions, and provide insights and information about the community. Depending on their expertise, available time, and interest, committee members should be willing to invest more in the project, perhaps by helping with interviews and soliciting financial and other support.

An advisory or planning committee is created not just for good public relations but also to carry out important work. Establish a democratic process for considering all ideas and try to reach a consensus about the project's direction. Even though it may be easier to "do it myself," time invested in a group effort will, in the long run, benefit the project and community. Through cooperation, the committee will be able to consider multiple views regarding goals and approaches, will become committed to completing the project, and will be better prepared to initiate and support future community history projects.

Collaborative work involves both benefits and pitfalls. Committees usually offer liberal advice and criticism but are more reluctant to raise money, follow through on promises, and share their load of project responsibilities. Many times, people agree to serve on committees but then do not find time to attend meetings or donate their labor. When approaching individuals to serve on a committee, ask if they can make a serious commitment to the project and regularly attend scheduled meetings or contribute in meaningful ways. Impress upon your committee members the seriousness of their task, but also stress the rewards involved with community history and cooperative work. It may be constructive to establish guidelines for committee members' continued participation, such as establishing a minimum number of meetings attended sequentially or participation in subcommittee work. This allows all potential members to understand from the beginning the commitment involved.

Project Planning Procedures

At the initial advisory committee meeting review the goals of a historical project and the distinctive characteristics of oral history before the group brainstorms project ideas. Some training and specific directions will help committee members understand the value and purpose of oral history, the difficulties and pleasures associated with interviewing, and the resources required for a project. For subsequent meetings, establish clear agenda items and guide discussions so that everyone participates and all topics are deliberated in a timely fashion. Following the sessions, summarize discussions and decisions and promptly distribute the results to the committee. If committee members are constantly kept abreast of project progress, planners can avoid misunderstandings that arise from a lack of communication.

Include volunteers and paid staff, such as interviewers and transcribers, in the planning process. If project participants assist with planning, they will have a greater understanding of and commitment to the project goals. They will want to get to know and learn from the advisory committee, and the committee can benefit from volunteer/staff ideas and suggestions.

While an advisory or project committee will contribute new ideas, problems may multiply as the committee expands. If your group seems too unwieldy, you may want to divide the group into smaller working committees to oversee and implement various parts of the project.

Community Relations

Trust is an essential component of any oral history project. Especially in community history, the success of future projects rides on the initial project's rapport with community members. Maintaining good relations involves upholding promises and demonstrating sensitivity to community concerns. Obviously, newcomers or outside researchers will achieve only limited success if they fail to establish a trusting relationship with individuals involved in a project; even those who are insiders are still accountable for the manner and spirit in which a project is conducted. Community projects require attention to and observance of oral history ethics, as outlined in the Oral History Association's *Evaluation Guidelines* (see Suggested Resources).

The advisory committee can play a key role in selecting the most important person associated with a community project—the project director. Most community projects find it helpful to hire or appoint someone to direct or coordinate the project and ensure that all the work gets done. Sometimes having one person "in charge" to keep tabs on the interview process, to serve as liaison between various participants, to coordinate meetings, to secure grant funding, and to answer questions can be the key to actually completing a project. This person has to be both highly responsible and well regarded in the community. As the sample projects in Section 3 reveal, project directors might be volunteers from the community, graduate students or researchers interested in the community's history, or paid professionals.

Selecting a Project Director, Staff, and Volunteers

Most community projects must rely on volunteer efforts for much or all of their work, and so developing professionalism among volunteers and obtaining commitments to see the project through completion become essential. You can draw on your committee members to publicize the project to find volunteers for a variety of tasks, or contact appropriate organizations to help with recruitment, such as a local conservation association for an oral history project on a park. While it is important to recruit as many interested volunteers as possible, a few dedicated, talented, and reliable individuals will be of greater value to the project than a roomful of initially enthusiastic supporters who gradually lose interest in the project. (Section 2 of this pamphlet, "Problems Common to Community Projects," provides additional suggestions for retaining your volunteers.)

Although it is necessary to have one person in charge, a project director or coordinator should avoid making lone decisions. Involve the planning committee and volunteers in hiring the project staff or in assigning duties. Volunteers and staff often become discouraged with oral history projects because of the solitary nature of the work. Off alone interviewing or transcribing, personnel rarely have an opportunity to come together. The project committee should plan to meet frequently to discuss progress, evaluate interviews, and share each other's findings and concerns. This welcome interaction also serves to reinvigorate everyone in the next stages of the project.

Community oral history projects often begin with great enthusiasm but quickly lose steam when participants become frustrated and lose interest in the ambitious aims of their project. A chief cause of that frustration stems from a lack of clearly understood and feasible goals. Once an advisory committee is formed and project personnel assembled, discuss and outline your goals. You may want to review and discuss a checklist such as the following:

Establishing Project Objectives

- What are the project objectives?

- How do you intend to accomplish them?

- Where do you plan to obtain funding?

- Will this be the first of many projects or a single effort to document the community's past?

- What community historical research and oral history interviews have already been done?

- How can this work be incorporated into the project you are planning?

- How many interviews do you hope to produce?

- When can they realistically be completed?

- What will become of the completed recordings? How will they be processed, preserved, and made accessible to others?

- Will you search for other historical materials, such as photographs, documents, artifacts, and memorabilia, while interviewing? If so, how?

- Do you plan to create a community oral history archives? If so, how?

- How will the interviews be used (e.g., to instruct schoolchildren, museum visitors, or another special audience; to be excerpted in a publication or in a series of radio broadcasts; etc.)?

It is important to ask these and other questions and to discuss project goals with your committee before launching a project. Your group may want to consult with a professional, such as an historian or folklorist from the local university, or to attend an oral history workshop to receive additional guidance. Many regional historical societies, oral history associations, and university oral history programs offer periodic workshops.

The community oral history project's specific focus will help shape a work plan. A project's intent to explore the post-1940s changes in a neighborhood's ethnic composition or the impact of 1960s urban renewal programs on a city will indicate how many interviews will be needed to adequately tell the story of the community and the period.

A specific plan will be required for any kind of grant proposal or funding request to support the community oral history project. Even if your committee has the resources to begin a project without outside support, it is imperative to outline objectives thoroughly and adhere to a work plan that project organizers agree upon. Such self-discipline will be appreciated in the long run, and your committee and community will feel a sense of accomplishment when goals are met on schedule.

Many times, constraints of resources and/or time will determine the scope of the project. When planning, consider the availability of both human and financial resources. How many interviewers, transcribers, and other support staff can you count on to help with the project? Will they volunteer their efforts or do they require compensation? Many costs may be eliminated with institutional support from a library, museum, or school, which may offer the project office space, telephones, copy machines, computers, and other equipment. Weigh your projected costs against potential income and donated supplies and services. A realistic budget will indicate how many interviews a group can afford to produce.

Budget and Scheduling

Time is another factor. If the oral history project is tied to a planned publication or anniversary deadline, allow plenty of time for research, interviewing, processing, and interpreting the inter-view material. Some oral historians estimate that it takes about thirty hours to produce a single one-hour recorded interview, when considering preparation, interviewing, and processing time. Despite digital recorders and computers that produce clearer sound record-ings, verbatim transcripts still require intensive labor, depending on the transcriber's efficiency. For some oral history projects, the work involved in processing interviews consumes a full half of the program's budget and time.

On the interviewing side, groups often fail to consider the amount of time needed to contact and gain the trust of prospective narra-tors. We sometimes assume that potential narrators will leap at the chance to be interviewed, agree to our proposed schedule, and discuss all topics within our projected two-hour interview slot. But people are not as predictable as our recording equipment. You may need and want to attend gatherings and events, visit with community leaders and prospective narrators, and observe community life before initiating a first interview.

Community expectations and cultural mores may also dictate patience. If you want to explore controversial historical topics, even more time is needed to gain trust and ensure that participants are not offended by your efforts. Interviewers should estimate how much time might be necessary to prepare for and produce interviews, and how long it will take to complete the desired number of interviews. A time cushion between the conclusion of interviews and the production of any scheduled final product will allow for inevitable delays.

Even if you do not have an imposed deadline, never leave a project timeline open-ended. If your group does not set a completion date, the project more than likely will fade into the background as other pressing matters take precedence.

Determining the Project Focus

At first glance, a community oral history project seems to have a built-in focus—the history of the community itself. Your community will present some obvious boundaries, in both time and space—the suburb was not created until 1947, the ethnic group settled the neighborhood after the 1950s, or a group of stonemasons practiced their craft just for a twenty-year period. But even a community as narrowly defined as a ten-block neighborhood or an ethnic group with recent immigrant roots suggests myriad questions and topics that could constitute many different projects. Many projects attempt to cover too much ground in too little time, trying to document the "whole" history of a community, such as the past one hundred years of a town or the history of all ethnic groups in a city. In many cases, these all-encompassing efforts outline a community's heritage in broad brush strokes for a commemorative event or publication. But oral history best serves the needs of historical research when it uncovers new information. Often this is accomplished by examining microcosmic events, such as 1950s desegregation efforts in one community, and ordinary experiences, such as work routines in the home, farm, or factory.

Narrowing the Project Focus

After establishing objectives, considering resource availability, and setting a schedule, the next step is to narrow the project's focus and agree upon a subject to pursue. The problem lies not with selecting a topic—there are dozens of themes your committee will be anxious to explore—but with developing a manageable focus that allows for thorough documentation of a fairly limited subject. A general guideline is to move from the general to the more specific when designing a comprehensive project. You may realize that a history of the town is too ambitious, so you develop a more realistic study of downtown and then further narrow the theme to women-run businesses.

One guideline for tightening a project's focus is the potential usefulness of the resulting interviews. A collection of recorded reminiscences covering everything from town businesses to impressions of a devastating flood is difficult to use. Interviews that just scratch the surface of a topic are of little historical value, and few researchers are willing to wade through interviews that explore multiple themes in less than thorough detail. Organized projects focusing on specific topics such as community institutions or a particular event or period are more inviting to potential researchers. A project entitled "The Brewing Industry of Milwaukee" or "The Choteau Woman's Club," for instance, is of more interest and potential use than something as general as "Milwaukee Pioneers" or "Women of Choteau."

An oral history project provides an opportunity to answer particular questions about a community's past. Why did Croatians settle on the east side of town and Slovenians on the west side? What explains the rise and decline of support for a local ball team? Consider what has characterized the community's past and development—schisms over controversial issues, annual community-wide celebrations and events, economic change, ethnic traditions, school consolidation, and so on.

Selecting a Topic

Too often community oral history projects overlap or duplicate much published and unpublished work on a popular topic. Avoid this kind of redundancy and concentrate instead on subjects that have been overlooked. Determine where gaps exist in written records and where oral history interviews might provide significant new information. A folklorist working in a small town in Mississippi, for instance, discovered that the bicentennial county history contained no mention of a local hospital owned and operated by African Americans from the late 1920s to the mid-1960s. Through oral history interviews, she was able to record a good deal of information about an institution that played a vital role in the lives of nearly half the town's population.

Check existing community history materials in libraries, schools, and archives at both the state and local levels to discover which topics have been well covered and which might need more work. The more you investigate, the more questions will come to mind. For example, from perusing the local newspapers from the 1940s, you may come across references to the activities of the Ku Klux Klan, but the reports lack detail. What was the extent of community participation in the Klan? Who supported and tolerated it? To what extent did it influence local politics and business? What were the reasons for its demise? Research is like detective work: only when you piece together jumbled bits of information can you begin the hunt for the missing pieces of the puzzle.

Consider what projects might be of most use and value in the long run. Many community history project planners believe their mission is to document community origins. But interest in the distant past need not rule the selection of a topic. Many contemporary themes and issues, such as a power line or dam construction controversy, technological change in local industry, or social phenomena like gentrification or homelessness, provide opportunities to record the still-vivid views of a variety of individuals. One project in southeastern Idaho, for example, recorded the impressions of survivors of the 1976 Teton Dam disaster. Professors and students from Ricks College and Utah State University and community volunteers asked residents about their experiences during and after the flood, its effects on their lives and communities, and folklore surrounding the event.

Sometimes project planners are attracted to the unusual events and personalities gracing a community's history or to residents' participation in celebrated events. Some may want to document people's memories of a celebrity, such as a movie star, sports figure, or politician, who spent childhood years in the community. While interesting, should celebrated individuals who gained fame and spent most of their lives outside the community be the subjects of an oral history project? How much will such interviews tell you about your community? Or your group may be interested in documenting certain World War II battles in which some townspeople participated. Should the focus of the project center on overseas experiences or on the effect of the war on the local home front? You may want to reorient the theme to explore specific community concerns, such as how rationing and shortages affected individuals and businesses, and how military service affected returning veterans' relationships, job opportunities, and lives in their community.

Your group can establish priorities for other topics to pursue once the original project is completed. There are dozens of themes that will strike you as important. Or an upcoming commemoration date might spur a particular project. Through a process of elimination, project planners can select one central topic or a series of closely related topics as the project focus. Each community member has a wealth of information about various subjects that will illuminate the historical record if the oral history project is well conceived, self-contained, and undertaken with specificity and direction.

Identifying Resources

Local Direct and In-kind Support

Community oral history project planners frequently ask: "How can we find financial support?" Adequate financing is crucial to every successful project, but a lack of money should not discourage any group, for there are many creative ways to find resources. In planning your project, create a realistic budget that estimates all necessary expenses, then locate funds to support that budget. Later you may have to scale down your project if sufficient resources cannot be obtained, but an initial budget clearly outlines needs and reminds participants of the expenses involved in an oral history project. With a well-conceived plan and budget, you will have better success in obtaining support.

Your most likely source of financial assistance is the community itself. Community backing can come in the form of both direct financial support and "in-kind" services—technical expertise, loaned equipment and office space, and donated supplies. Publicize your project, and announce your need for support. Explain how the project you have planned will benefit the community. Approach businesses, city government, the local historical society or museum, ethnic associations, schools, church groups, women's and civic clubs, labor unions, and individuals who may be able to assist you. Retired seniors might be willing to transcribe interviews, an electronics store might sell microphones at a discount, and a television station may be willing to donate some labor and equipment for editing recorded interviews. Every little bit helps, so accept with gratitude the smallest donation. Community investment in the project also translates into support and involvement in the project, as more people will feel a sense of ownership and will be interested in the project's outcome.

To be most successful, a community oral history project should have an institutional base. Not only is affiliation with a community institution—such as a library, college, or historical society—essential for obtaining grant funding, but an institution can provide otherwise expensive staffing, office space and other subsidies. In addition, institutional support can give a project legitimacy by allowing people to readily identify your project with a place. All an institution may ask for in return is that you list its name as a sponsor of the project on any publications or other products resulting from the project. In some communities, there are rivalries between competing institutions, but you can work this to your advantage by seeking sponsorship from all institutions. An outsider needs to be especially careful to solicit support from all available sources to avoid antagonizing any segment of the community. For any community project, the more participants the better, so try to line up support from all quarters—churches, unions, ethnic and civic associations, businesses, and historical and cultural groups. In a brochure or website describing the project and in other publicity, you can list sponsors and generate additional support by making your project truly community-wide.

Additional Funding

After first looking in your own backyard for support, you may want to seek outside funding from public and private sources within your state or region. Each community is unique and will have different financial resources at its disposal, and each state has a variety of public and private grant sources for funding special projects. Consult with individuals who frequently seek and obtain assistance or who are familiar with granting agency guidelines. These people might include the reference librarian at your public library, a grants manager at the local college or university, or a local arts program or museum successful in obtaining grants. On the state level, you could contact the state humanities and arts councils, the state oral historian or folklorist, and the state historical society and library. Find someone in your community with grant-writing experience to guide your committee in the process of finding sources and developing a proposal. State humanities councils and universities frequently sponsor grant-writing workshops. Attend the annual meeting of your state or regional oral history association where you can meet representatives from other community groups who have faced similar financial challenges and who can offer suggestions.

A state humanities council may be a logical source of funding, especially for developing public and media programs that result from your oral history project. Before developing and submitting a proposal, however, be sure to inquire about the council's past support of oral history. Each state humanities commission offers varying degrees of support for oral history. Some rarely grant money to such endeavors; others do so on a regular basis. It is best to consult with the staff of the council to discuss your project. Part of their job is to assist communities in preparing proposals.

Humanities proposals require specific work plans, the involvement of professional humanities scholars (often a local history professor), and detailed descriptions of how the community will be involved in the project and how the project will be evaluated. These requirements actually provide good guidelines for conceiving and executing a community oral history project. Humanities scholars can suggest research methods, draft pertinent interview questions, evaluate the collected materials, and provide guidance on interpretation. As with many public funding agencies which administer grants, these sources require a certain amount of paperwork and careful accounting, and groups seeking assistance must be prepared to devote time to grant administration.

Other public sources of support might include a state fund for cultural projects, re-granting agencies such as an arts commission, the state department of education, or other state agencies. Do not overlook private sources, such as individuals, associations, corporations, and foundations, which might be interested in your project. You may discover, for example, that the power company has a foundation for supporting community heritage and development projects, or a philanthropic resident has been known to donate money to groups pursuing issues such as your oral history topic. Approach groups that would logically have an interest in your project. For example, a professional teachers' association might be interested in supporting a project on a teacher's strike, rural schoolteachers, or 1960s student social movements.

Regardless of the amount of money you seek, do not be afraid to ask. Build a strong case for supporting your project. Break up financial needs into small chunks—such as specific amounts needed for transcribing or photo reproduction—which can be "sold" more easily to individual funding sources. Most of your requests may be denied, but your persistence will eventually yield a return.

Along with project personnel, choosing the right equipment for your project can be critical to its success. Think of the final recording as the culmination of many hours of labor, an irreplaceable, priceless treasure, whose audibility and longevity ought to be guaranteed. With a little bit of effort and expense, you can make certain that your recordings are of the highest possible quality and valuable to future generations.

Selecting Equipment

Oral historians have become increasingly concerned about producing high-quality sound recordings. In community projects, where the final recordings will most likely be used in some kind of media format, such as radio, exhibits, or webcasts, it is imperative to locate and use good recording equipment. As of this writing, most projects have embraced digital recorders. Flash memory recorders have become standard field recorders and are relatively easy to use. Digital audio can be transferred to and used in different mediums, such as websites and PowerPoint presentations. After a recording session, the interviewer transfers the WAV file from the recorder's memory card to the project's computer hard disk. The sound recording will be a file on the computer. It cannot be emphasized enough that you should make back up files onto another hard drive and/or CD. Despite the turn to digital recordings, some oral history projects continue to rely on standard cassette tape recorders for recording and/or preservation to match the format used by the collecting institution.

Technological concerns and preferences are constantly shifting and therefore specific recommendations are beyond the scope of this pamphlet. A few suggestions endure, however, regardless of changes in technology. First, you do not need to purchase the most expensive recorder on the market, but it should be of high quality. Next, the recording quality of any recorder can be improved by a good external microphone, which can block out external noises and amplify the voice of your narrator. Many external microphones require batteries, and interviewers must take caution to insert fresh batteries periodically. Lapel or lavaliere microphones that can be clipped onto a narrator's shirt are unobtrusive and can significantly improve the sound quality of a recording. If you interview more than one person, however, each will need a separate lapel mike, which can be joined together in an adapter that fits your recorder's microphone jack.

Seek additional equipment advice. Technicians at your local music and electronics store or your public radio station, or the state oral historian or folklorist will be able to guide you. The oral history listserv, H-ORALHIST http://www.h-net.org/~oralhist/, provides the best and most current recommendations about recorders, microphones, and preservation of recordings. A member of the H-Net, Humanities & Social Sciences On-Line initiative, H-Oralhist is a network for oral historians, many of whom regularly post equipment advice.

While high quality equipment is essential, of equal importance is your ability to use it correctly. Practice with your equipment before conducting your first interview. The best equipment in the world will not cover up an interviewer's unfamiliarity with settings, cords, and switches, or improper set-up and operation of the machine. Novice and experienced interviewers alike are often surprised and dismayed to discover that their painstakingly recorded interview is inaudible because the volume was set too low, the digital recorder full and unable to record additional sound, the microphone accidentally covered, batteries dead, or the pause button never released. Review an equipment checklist before each interview to make certain that equipment operates smoothly, and that you have needed supplies. Feeling confident with your equipment and consistently repeating precautionary steps will help you conduct an interview comfortably and successfully.

Selecting Narrators for Your Project

Central to the community oral history project are appropriate narrators who can best shed light on your chosen topic. Most community projects have access to a host of such people who have lucid memories, are accomplished storytellers, and represent a range of perspectives. You can find them through various community contacts and by publicizing the project in the local media. Using these sources, you are likely to develop an extensive list of potential people to interview. Your problem then becomes one of selection so that the final collection of interviews is representative. Again, planning can help insure that your interviews as a body reflect the diversity of your particular community and that an adequate sample is obtained within imposed time or budgetary constraints.

A project's focus will determine the numbers and kinds of people you will want to contact. Compile a tentative list of narrators who were actual observers of or participants in the subject being documented. Eyewitnesses are the primary sources in oral history, rather than the "keepers" of community history who may have studied but not witnessed firsthand the event or experience in question. A local historian may have investigated thoroughly a major strike in 1946, but this knowledge will not be as compelling as that of the worker, labor organizer, or company manager directly involved in the event. In many cases, certain key narrators will be essential to the project, and all principal players should be interviewed if possible.

Also critical are prospective narrators who played secondary roles in or observed events from the sidelines. Do not limit your pool of interviews to visible figures—civic leaders, club presidents, union officers—but seek the viewpoints of middle managers, quiet activists, and the rank-and-file. A project documenting a transition in town government might include the insights of veteran city hall secretaries and other employees, defeated candidates as well as elected officials, and citizen group representatives. Project interviewers exploring the history of the Original Governor's Mansion in Helena, Montana, for example, found that some of their best information about the building came from former cooks, gardeners, and neighbors instead of governors and their spouses. Often, people who may be the least conspicuous are those who know best the inner workings of institutions and may be the keenest observers of events over time.

Sometimes crucial people are overlooked because a committee lacks contact or familiarity with all segments of a community. Planners may rely on the suggestions of individuals who know a variety of people in the community; the local historian, mayor, ethnic association president, and minister all have such knowledge. Some people, however, want to put the best face on the community and consciously or unconsciously recommend only prominent or conventional individuals to interview. But what of the seasonal worker, single mother, or political maverick? Their perspectives provide valuable insights into aspects of community life not usually examined.

A common belief among groups starting out an oral history project is that they must interview all the community's elders before they die. Certainly senior citizens are valuable informants facing a finite future with the passage of time. But if we think of each project as an opportunity to capture the impressions and views of different generations, the resulting information will be that much richer. Say, for example, your project on community recreation encompasses the period 1945 through 2000. You might locate individuals who were young in each of the six decades, including the contemporary generation of children, and ask all of them to discuss childhood games and play in your community. If your project is examining the history and activities of area women's organizations, you might want to talk to recent joiners as well as long-time members.

As interviewing gets underway, the group's tentative list of narrators will undoubtedly change. Interviewers will come across additional people with particularly keen insights or important perspectives, and some prospective narrators will prove to be inaccessible or uncooperative. Sometimes community projects face the touchy issue of maintaining community support while practicing selectivity. Community members may complain about other individuals being interviewed although they themselves feel they have more significant stories to tell. Planners will need to explain the selection process, pointing out the costs and time involved with oral history that limit the number of interviews that can be produced. They also can encourage people to interview their own family members and neighbors, and thus become involved, even if indirectly, in the project. As with all stages of the project, planners will find that flexibility is necessary. In most community projects there are abundant potential narrators who will be eager or willing to share their reminiscences.

Preparing to Interview

Preparation for an effective interview begins long before the interviewer is face-to-face with the narrator. A project committee might include a special committee on research to survey available source materials and distill their research into background summaries and topical outlines for use in interviews. Project consultants or humanities scholars could direct the research effort or suggest methods and resources. Informed interviewers are better able to ask probing and relevant questions and understand the significance of information offered by the narrator. Adequate preparation includes researching all available sources that might illuminate the subject(s) to be broached in the interview. The interviewer need not become an expert on the topic, but should know enough to feel comfortable asking a broad range of questions related to it and not duplicate on tape what is already in print.

Written sources, both primary and secondary, can provide broad outlines for your subject and will raise unanswered questions that you can pursue in your interviews. This kind of research can serve as a road map for guiding the interviewer to areas to explore; once there, the interviewer can venture into terrain not visible on such a map.

A good place to start in your general research is with the products of other community history projects. A book or article about a northeastern urban neighborhood may seem to have little in common with a rural southern town, but the planners of the southern project may find the northeastern study a source of applicable ideas and pertinent questions. You may want to turn to other sources that have no direct bearing on your particular community but that will highlight important concepts to consider.

For example, written histories of Italian Americans in other parts of the US will offer ideas to the group documenting Italian Americans in Rock Springs, Wyoming, or Greenville, Mississippi.

In your research, you will naturally consult published sources that may concern your topic. Community newspapers and local histories will provide important background information even if not directly linked to your subject. Historical society archives and libraries have primary sources, such as original records, manuscripts, written and oral reminiscences that will also be helpful in your search. Many of these records are now available online through the Internet, including institutional websites, state and local genealogical home pages, or for-profit or free sites such as http://www.ancestry.com or http://www.rootsweb.com.

Creativity is fundamental for this kind of research. A search in library catalogs, indexes, or databases for information on migrant workers in South Bend, Indiana, for example, may turn up few sources. But one can locate employment and educational statistics, reports on housing conditions, and even brief histories and biographies from such agencies as the state department of employment and the Indiana Migrant Council. Churches and associations may have additional helpful information, such as scrapbooks, logs of activities, and meeting minutes. Other information may come from the papers of governors or legislators interested in migrant worker issues or records from the state department of agriculture.

Whether you plan to focus your project on local social movements of the 1950s or a regional environmental controversy of the 1990s, there are numerous secondary sources on related subjects that will assist you in drafting outlines of topics to cover in your interviews. This research is critical, too, for placing the community project within a larger historical context.

Knowledge about regional and national developments can illuminate the fact that seemingly local events did not exist in isolation and can expand an oral history project's scope to address wider concerns and to invite comparative judgments. Anti-poverty programs of the 1960s were not unique to your community—how did they compare with other communities' programs? How did support for or objections to the federal projects correspond to the general mood of the country at the time? Most contemporary issues parallel similar developments in other communities. How does a regional controversy such as the logging of old growth forests in the Pacific Northwest relate to economic and environmental fears in other single-industry communities of the 1980s?

Do not let the lack of written materials on your topic deter you from background research. Nontraditional sources and a community's folklife can offer rich background materials. Church services, weekend dances, public murals, annual celebrations, or traditional meals all provide clues to understanding a community's history. Narrators themselves, in pre-interview conversations, can provide valuable information from their own backgrounds or observations of events, or may have materials that might help with your research, such as journals, photographs, scrapbooks, letters, or other records.

As your research nears completion, develop an interview outline or subject list. You will find that the more you investigate a topic, the more questions will occur to you. Gaps in the record or puzzling comments will prompt a quest for more details. Tantalizing passages such as "a lively discussion ensued" or "a plant explosion killed five people" offer the interviewer specific leads to pursue in interviews.

Such an interview guide, outline, or subject list offers the interviewer a critical tool. If several interviewers are working on the same project, the topical outlines will insure that the project results have some consistency. Much can be learned from how many different people answer the same question. However, an interview outline should not include specific questions, but suggest general themes and topics to explore. If you are interviewing first-generation immigrants, for example, you probably do not need a list of specific questions such as, "When did you come to this country? Why did you immigrate? By what method did you travel? Who came with you?" Notes as general as "immigration" or other key words or phrases may be enough to trigger numerous questions about the circumstances surrounding immigration without limiting the interviewer to prepared questions that may stifle spontaneity. More specific guidelines for constructing interview outlines and conducting interviews can be found in other oral history manuals (see Suggested Resources).

Processing and Disseminating the Final Product

Storage and Processing

Community oral history projects have a responsibility to make their end results, the recorded interviews, available to the public. Early in planning, the committee should decide where to deposit the interview recordings, legal releases, and accompanying project materials. The planning committee might include a librarian or archivist from the repository where the interviews will be donated who can offer suggestions about which recording formats will be most appropriate, whether analog tape or digital file, and how to identify, describe, and process the interviews. The library or archive may have its own legal release form to use and specific formats for processing and accessioning the interviews. If this is the case, it will be important to find out about and obtain the release forms prior to beginning the interviews, so you will not have to re-contact narrators to obtain their signed forms after the interviews.

A crucial stage of any oral history project is processing the recording. Satisfied that so many good interviews have been recorded, many groups put them away for safekeeping without publicizing their existence or providing finding aids for their use. But few researchers are willing to listen to hours of recordings with no indication of the kinds of information they contain. When planning the project, allow plenty of time for preparing user guides to the interviews. At the very least, provide an index to the recordings, that is, a list or description of subjects discussed in the interview. Even more useful are detailed summaries of each five-minute segment of the recording. With more time, money, or volunteers, projects can produce verbatim transcripts of the interviews. Transcripts can be bound or posted online for convenient use and are the preferred format for most oral history programs and repositories. Transcripts are especially helpful to researchers or groups using the interviews for publications and public programs.

Special attention must be devoted to the care and storage of the recorded interviews, so that these valuable reminiscences are preserved indefinitely. We encourage you to consult one of the several good manuals available that address in detail how to store interviews, and to review the latest discussions of the same on H-Oralhist. More important, find and work with a local or regional repository that is willing and able to care for your interviews and related materials.

The ultimate purpose of any oral history project, of course, is to increase understanding of the past. Together, project planners and repositories can encourage use of the materials by publicizing the project, making recordings and transcripts readily available, and creating inexpensive guides, websites, or brochures about the collection. Easy access encourages appreciation for and interest in a community's past and generates support for additional oral history projects.

Disseminating the Results

An accepted principle of community history is to share findings of your project with the community. This is an intimidating step for many historians, because their interpretations are presented to the community for immediate reaction. But generating community response—both good and bad—is one of the true joys of community history work. Community members can actively participate in critiquing the work in a number of public forums, where they can respond to the project's findings and interpretations.

Interpretation

Besides making tapes and transcripts available for others to use, project organizers may be inspired to use the materials themselves to create interpretive products such as publications, films, websites, and exhibits. Just as the project's focus guided the interview questions, so will the project objectives steer evaluation of the oral interviews. Do you plan to write a book? Produce a play? Design an exhibit? Make a film? Will you need to select verbatim interview excerpts or make some general conclusions? Your plans for presenting the findings from your project will influence how much of the interview materials to interpret.

The most challenging and interesting portion of a project is sifting through the interviews, looking for patterns and themes. You will find that as few as half a dozen interviews offer numerous interpretive possibilities. Perhaps you will discover that oral accounts of an event differ in some important respect from written reports. The comparison between them can be instructive and illuminating. Or you might find that the interviews contradict one another. For example, residents of one urban neighborhood had very different memories of how an urban renewal project affected their community. Sometimes the new information generated by the oral histories can fundamentally alter the community's own sense of itself. Convinced for years that their town's only industry closed because of new strict environmental regulations and unreasonable union demands, one community's residents began to question this assumption when confronted with the first-hand stories of company mismanagement, union-busting, polluting activities, and capital reinvestment in a Latin American country.

Programs and Presentations

One of the easiest and most inexpensive ways to present oral history excerpts is through existing community channels, such as the local newspaper or radio station. A series of articles or transcript excerpts might be produced for the newspaper, and selections of interview recordings, with a brief introduction, could be used on the public service portion of commercial radio stations; longer pieces could be developed for the public radio station. If your final recordings are of good sound and content quality, local media will welcome programs and articles. Look for other readily available vehicles: perhaps the local chamber of commerce is preparing brochures about your community that could benefit from some oral history excerpts, or high school social studies classes may be looking for primary source material for an upcoming project.

Your group may plan to produce a more ambitious work such as a book. Most community publications follow one of two models: grouping selected oral history excerpts around specific themes with a general introduction, or presenting an interpretive narrative that incorporates excerpts from interviews. Some community history booklets include a description of the project's methodology and instructions for how to execute a similar oral history project.

If your local historical society is planning to write a community history, make sure it is aware of the results of the oral history project. Sometimes writers are wary of using interview material, questioning oral history's reliability and fearing that interviews are more difficult to wade through than traditional written sources. The many excellent community oral history publications available can assuage the fears of doubters and demonstrate how oral history can enliven any publication, and they may serve as models or generate ideas for aspiring authors.

Even more accessible than publications are media and public programs that reach a wide, diverse audience. Although requiring a much greater expense than a simple publication or an effort subsidized by a local radio station, these productions are usually more easily funded than strictly archival oral history projects because they are more visible and likely can generate public support. Often podcasts, films, or websites appeal to younger generations and successfully communicate information through the voices of narrators and the images of historic sites, artifacts, and people working on the job, in the home, and with handicrafts. One Native American woman in Montana interviewed Sioux quilters from the Fort Peck Reservation and produced a media program juxtaposing images of the colorful and unique star quilts with the voices of their makers. If your group can videotape interviews, a producer has even a wider range of choices in splicing together historic and contemporary images for a program.

Exhibits of photographs and artifacts used in conjunction with oral history excerpts offer a means of disseminating information to diverse audiences without the personnel and equipment required of media programs. Once an exhibit is produced, especially if it is designed to travel, it can be installed at a site and left freestanding without much supervision. A particularly effective use of oral history in exhibitions involves recorded excerpts that either play continuously or are activated when the viewer/listener pushes a button or picks up a telephone receiver. The Idaho State Historical Society's traveling exhibit on Idaho small towns featured such recorded selections along with mounted photographs and an accompanying booklet.

Walking tours, site interpretations, and dramatic productions are other possibilities for showcasing community oral histories. Project planners can work in tandem with historic preservationists to document the history of a site or district and use the oral sources to tell the human story of a building's or neighborhood's history. The Metropolitan Interfaith Association in Memphis, Tennessee, interviewed former and current residents of Cherokee, one of the city's predominantly African-American neighborhoods. The project sought to revitalize the neighborhood by increasing awareness of community history, and produced books and radio programs from the oral histories. As an indirect result, neighborhood preservationists were able to place several buildings on the National Register of Historic Places.

Dramatic productions can range from a simple reader's theater that involves residents as participants to a more elaborate stage production with professional writers and actors. The Vigilante Players, based at Montana State University in Bozeman, created a script from the oral histories of residents of Montana's smelter towns and then performed the play in those communities as well as throughout the state. The Great North American History Theatre of St. Paul, Minnesota, has used oral history in its productions, including the play *Down to Earth,* about a small Midwestern farming town during the Great Depression.

Your group may decide that since you have a wealth of information and captivating reminiscences, you want to work your material into a variety of programs. A different committee, including technical and scholarly advisors, can be formed to tackle this phase of the community oral history project. Several publications, including journals like *The Oral History Review* and books addressing specific kinds of public programs, offer ideas and instructions for designing and completing these kinds of final products.

Whatever the medium, it is important to think of accessible places to present your work. This will vary community to community, and planners should be aware of the variety of places where targeted audiences congregate. A neighborhood school may seem like a logical place to display an exhibit, until you realize that few adults will see it there. Similarly, do not assume that all community members are likely to visit the local museum. Shopping malls, courthouses, senior and community centers, libraries, parks, factory entrances, and other public and workplace spaces can reach the variety of people you hope will view the exhibit. The same holds true for other planned media and public programs. Figure out where members of your community traditionally congregate, and take your program to them. You may have a successful presentation by inviting the community to attend a free event at a public place such as a theater or community center, but don't limit your programs to these venues. Take your show on the road, to schools, union halls, and church, ethnic and civic groups. Make a celebration out of the opening of your oral history exhibit, play, or film. Send invitations, offer food and drink, and have an organized public discussion following the showing of your program. The working-class community of Anaconda, Montana, for example, held a hot-dog-and-beer reception for the opening of a photo/oral history exhibit on Montana's smelter towns. Visitors were encouraged to bring memorabilia, photos, and artifacts; one former smelterman showed historical slides of the plant and the town. The participants enjoyed the event immensely and later encouraged their families and neighbors to see the exhibit, thus generating an interest in the program that might not otherwise have existed.

The ways in which you can interpret and present your oral history interviews in publicly accessible formats are by no means limited to the suggestions offered here. The range of products you can create from oral histories is limited only by your imagination.

2

PROBLEMS COMMON TO COMMUNITY ORAL HISTORY PROJECTS

Following the steps we have suggested for planning and carrying out a community oral history project should make the entire process relatively smooth. Some problems in doing oral history on the community level turn up repeatedly, like the proverbial bad penny. In this section we describe some of the most common difficulties encountered and suggest ways of dealing with them.

Reinventing the Wheel

One of the most common problems in community oral history projects stems from failing to investigate what has already been done. Novice researchers may be unaware of state or regional historical depositories containing interviews, photographs, maps, written records, or books concerning their community. Professionals, too, can overlook community resources by researching only in major archival collections and scholarly literature. Careful detective work can lead to a surprising amount of information that will save you time and help you to focus on gaps in historical accounts. Systematic research can also help to correct erroneous information that may have been perpetuated in previous publications. The following scenario suggests how a local researcher who first starts to "reinvent the wheel" discovers the need to refocus his project:

> John Rodriguez decides to conduct an interview project on his county's role in the sheep industry. He first checks records available in the local library, and then contacts people who were major leaders in the sheep industry. One of the prospective narrators tells him that he was previously interviewed about this topic. John then tries to locate the interview. He is directed to the state historical archives where he finds a substantial interview collection and a book on the sheep industry. Both cover much of his research topic. John decides to reevaluate his project focus. The state archivist directs him to other sources of information within his community. His local librarian also helps him find and obtain books and articles written on his topic.

> Through these sources John discovers that, while much had been written on major leaders in the state's sheep industry, little was known about immigrants who herded the sheep. The Basque people played an important role in his community's history and a project focusing on their experiences had already been produced.

Virtually nothing, however, was known about the Portuguese who also herded the sheep. He enlists the help of a second-generation Portuguese-American woman, Mary Silva, who introduces him to the community. Together, they conduct further research particular to Portuguese immigration and settlement, attend Portuguese-American social functions, and gain access to personal and family records.

John and Mary learn, contrary to information that had been previously published, that neither the Basques nor the Portuguese had traditionally herded sheep in their homelands. They also discover the important role Basque and Portuguese women had played in family and local economies by running boardinghouses and restaurants. They uncover instances of prejudice against the immigrant groups when they first settled. They study how the two ethnic groups assimilated into the local culture, yet kept some of their traditions alive—information not covered in previous local histories. John and Mary re-examine the research materials already collected and conduct interviews about specific topics. They produce a written report that highlights this "new" information and recommend future projects related to newer immigrants that recently worked as herders, such as Peruvians and others of South American descent.

This example shows why it is worth the extra research effort to avoid reinventing the wheel. If all research avenues are explored, if the information uncovered is analyzed and followed up for more details, then a new and valuable study can be produced. Work like John and Mary's could contribute significantly to the group's understanding of their heritage as well as to local, state, and national history.

More than likely, an individual or group initiating a community oral history project has some connection with the community under study—as members of the neighborhood, ethnic community, or occupational group.

"Insider" versus "Outsider" Interviewers

In many ways, there are advantages to being an insider to the community. You have a personal familiarity with the people and the area that would take an outsider a long time to cultivate, you probably know where to look for historical records within your community, and you understand the culture and mores of the community and its relationship to other communities.

Because of your own membership in the community, however, you may be hampered by your own assumptions, experiences, and attitudes as a member of that group. Some of the difficulties you may encounter include:

- soliciting perspectives other than your own, or even recognizing that the community may encompass members from different backgrounds than your own;

- injecting your own experiences and anecdotes into the interview because of your familiarity with the community;

- failing to question statements or letting references to places and past events pass without elaboration, and thus limiting the amount of information recorded for future researchers.

Personal relationships can also affect interview quality. For example, you know what kinds of information and stories older members of your family can provide. On the other hand, you may have heard them so often that you may not ask about them again or follow up on the details. In some instances, painful episodes in the family or community's past may constrain your line of questioning. If you have a close relationship with a narrator or the community more generally, you may hesitate to probe more deeply.

There are also special pressures incumbent on "insider" community historians to present only the positive aspects of the community. It is natural to promote your own group and celebrate its endurance and at the same time to overlook the darker side of community life or discord between its members. Insiders have to continue to live within the group after the project is completed and may depend on the good will of others to support their work. Thus, there is a tendency to focus interviews only on the positive aspects of community life and instances of solidarity and homogeneity. The "we" that represents the community as a whole in the interview is not defined; aphorisms and platitudes such as "we were all in the same boat" or "we took care of our own" are not clarified or explained.

Creating a more honest rather than just a celebratory history takes considerable awareness, tact, and preparation on the part of any interviewer. Interviewers should not avoid conflicts and divisions in a community's past but find ways to explore them with narrators. An insider can avoid touching sensitive nerves by carefully explaining why such information needs to be included, and by following legal and ethical guidelines in the public presentation of such information. And including a variety of individuals in the project will help insure that multiple perspectives are revealed.

It is also common for "outsiders" to initiate community projects, particularly students and scholars who recognize the uniqueness or importance of a town, neighborhood, or group. As an outsider to a community, you can bring a fresh perspective to its history. Since you do not have the same kind of intimate knowledge of a group as an insider, you may ask about things an insider takes for granted. Sometimes as an interested newcomer you can elicit more details and probe more sensitive issues than an insider simply because you are not involved in internal politics. An outsider may be able to identify a less well-known topic or other community members to be included in the research.

Some "outside" historians rush into a community eager to uncover its history and are surprised when they are met with suspicion, if not downright hostility. Unfortunately, this reaction may be caused by a community group's previous experience with an unethical or insensitive researcher who has not respected their experiences and perspectives. Outside researchers working closely with a community group may make the mistake of insisting on a project focus that had previously been rejected by its members. The outsider usually meets more success by listening to what community representatives consider most important and being willing to consider their suggestions.

As an outside researcher, you should make every effort to understand community culture and be respectful of it in contacting narrators and conducting interviews. The following advice is key to conducting a successful interview project as an "outsider":

- Represent yourself honestly, but refrain from giving offense to community members through inappropriate dress, language, or behavior;

- Use restraint in expressing your own political opinions and beliefs, or you may run the risk of offending certain members of the community whom you wish to interview in the future.

The following scenario (based on an actual incident) shows what can happen if someone does not attempt to understand or blend in with the community under study:

Jim Smith was hired by the Forest Service to conduct interviews in several remote timber communities. Though he had a strong background in anthropology, he had never conducted oral interviews or worked with community groups. He attempted to use public transportation to get to the area, but ended up hitchhiking and camping because public transportation and local hotels were limited. After several days he arrived, unkempt and unannounced, in one small town. He began knocking on doors and asking questions. Naturally, people were suspicious of him because of his appearance and ties to a locally unpopular federal agency. He also tended to argue with people over timber harvests, which afforded the basic livelihood of the community. Consequently, he was unsuccessful in obtaining any interviews. The Forest Service then hired two researchers who had previously conducted successful community oral history projects. These researchers made initial contacts with appropriate community representatives, then wrote and called prospective narrators. Many local residents were reluctant to be interviewed because of their previous experience with Jim Smith, but with patience and tact the researchers were able to complete several good interviews.

All outside researchers working independently on a project need to make initial contacts with community members. You should enter a locale aware of the work that has already been done and cognizant of community members who have been involved in that work, such as the local historian. That individual may not be someone you will need to interview, but he or she may open the doors of other local residents for you. Other good intermediaries are librarians, newspaper reporters, and public officials. All community members who provide you with assistance should be publicly recognized and thanked in your final product.

Whether you are an insider or an outsider to a community, finding narrators and conducting interviews require genuine interest and considerable skill in working with people. Sensitivity, respect, and a willingness to learn are the hallmarks of a good interviewer— whether you have lived in the community all your life or are an outsider entering it for the first time.

Volunteer and Narrator Burnout

All community oral history project directors must take care not to exhaust the human resources on which they depend. Both volunteer committee members and narrators can suffer from "burnout," and may quit or wish not to be involved in future projects. If a project is well conceived and planned, and project goals are established by group consensus, you are already on the right track to avoid this problem. The following are guidelines that can help prevent burnout:

- Make sure volunteers have a clear idea of what their roles are and have the appropriate skills to fulfill their roles. Develop a job description for each volunteer and review it carefully together to help ensure that everyone knows what is expected right from the start. A job description also helps both the volunteer and project director to ascertain whether this is the appropriate activity for his or her skills.

- Try to guide someone who is not a good listener to something other than interviewing; there are certainly plenty of other necessary tasks! Other jobs include helping with research, transferring recordings to hard drives and disks and creating files, indexing the interview, transcribing, proofreading the transcripts, cataloging the oral history collection, or selecting interview materials for a final product such as a website or exhibition. In any job description, identify not only the responsibilities, but also the rewards of doing this particular work. Indicate the kinds of assistance volunteers will receive and facilities they can use. In turn, ask for an estimated weekly commitment of time. Many local nonprofit agencies have such volunteer job descriptions, so borrow some samples to create your own.

- Once you have recruited volunteers, conduct training sessions to help them fulfill their job requirements. This is especially important if they will be conducting interviews for the first time. You can conduct the sessions yourself, or ask someone familiar with volunteer efforts to lead the workshops. The training sessions may weed out a few volunteers who discover the work is not what they had anticipated. Try to show them other job possibilities within the project; if they still wish to decline, thank them for their interest and encourage them to volunteer elsewhere.

- For those volunteers who decide to stay with the project, be sure to set short-term and long-term goals with them. Tracking progress toward goals and recognizing their achievement helps to keep both project directors and volunteers enthusiastic, as well as ensuring ongoing communication about goals. Tracking also keeps the focus of the project clear and the overall work on schedule. Set short-term goals that all can achieve easily, and celebrate those achievements.

- Be sure to recognize each volunteer's efforts. Simple notes of appreciation, an article in the local paper, or a more formal recognition party are all ways of doing so. Often the project director is the only one who receives public attention; highlight a particularly outstanding volunteer or at least make sure you mention the role of volunteers in every public forum.

- Above all, be patient and flexible. Do not forget that volunteers have lives beyond your project and are not being paid for their work. You do not have to tolerate undependable or uncooperative people, but try to keep your expectations reasonable.

Narrators pose a different kind of burnout problem, particularly when they have been interviewed numerous times about similar topics. Some narrators become irritated when they are asked about the same subjects repeatedly, and they may develop pat answers or offer streamlined accounts that contain no significant detail or insights. Both symptoms can affect the project's standing in the community and the quality of the information that is recorded, for unhappy narrators do not encourage others to be interviewed.

If you have done your homework, you will have checked all available oral history collections to see who has been previously interviewed on what topics. This does not mean, however, that knowledgeable sources should be ignored just because they have been previously interviewed, but their interviews should cover new ground. Get past the set pieces and ask for explanations, details, more personal experiences and insights. After the interviews, be sure to thank the narrators and see that each receives a copy of the recording or transcript.

Legal and Ethical Concerns

In a sense, all the issues in this pamphlet are ethical concerns, for community oral history projects require respect for human beings and their rights. Too often, though, researchers new to the field of oral history may not be aware of the ethical and legal implications of recording personal reminiscences and making them available to the public. We recommend that every project acquire copies of the Oral History Association's *Evaluation Guidelines,* available on its website http://www.dickinson.edu/oha. Periodically updated by the Association, these guidelines outline responsibilities and obligations of interviewers and projects to narrators and communities.

The key issues that community projects need to consider are: 1) the need for legal releases; 2) the need to handle controversial or damaging information with caution; 3) the responsibility to return the information gathered to the narrators and the community at large; and 4) the need to consider whether monetary compensation is appropriate.

1. Acquire a narrator's written permission to allow public access to the interview. According to current copyright law, the ownership of an oral history interview is shared by its co-creators. Ownership can be transferred to a third party, such as a library or an archive, with written authorization (usually

referred to as a legal release form). Numerous available publications deal with this issue. *Oral History and the Law,* by John Neuenschwander, another pamphlet in the Oral History Association Pamphlet Series, discusses legal concerns, including dilemmas posed by new technologies, and provides examples of current release forms (see Suggested Resources). Even in the case of small, informal community projects (and even if the project involves friends and family), a release must be obtained if the interviews are going to be made available to the public in a library or historical society collection or interpreted in media form. When developing your oral history project, you should consult sample legal releases included in most oral history manuals and on many websites. Some community groups include lawyers on their advisory committee; sometimes free legal advice is made available to nonprofit organizations through the auspices of a state bar association. After you have studied the examples or received some professional advice, design a release that best fits your situation.

Many volunteer interviewers hesitate to use legal releases because they are afraid narrators will refuse to sign them. If at the outset you explain carefully the purpose of your project, describe what will happen to the interview once it has been recorded, emphasize the valuable contribution that an individual's reminiscences can make to the project, and explain that you need written permission to include the interview in the project collection, then you probably will not be turned down. Occasionally, interviewers ask the narrator to sign a release before the interview, but it is usually more appropriate to explain the project goals and intended use of the interview before recording occurs, then ask the narrator to sign the release after the interview is completed. In any case, be sure that the release is obtained.

Never record secretly. Such conduct is not only highly unethical, but also in most cases illegal.

2. Be aware of issues of slander and libel when conducting interviews and making them publicly accessible. The *American Heritage Dictionary* defines slander as a false or malicious statement or report that damages the reputation or well-being of another. Libel is a written, printed, or pictorial statement that unjustly damages a person's reputation. Though it is rare for community projects to receive lawsuit threats concerning slander and libel, there is a danger of some historical accounts causing social injury to families and reopening community wounds. The line between community history and community gossip is sometimes thin, and troubling events that may seem long ago to one person may be painfully recent to another.

Communication is again the key to a successful project. If you transcribe the interviews, make sure the narrator has the opportunity to review and correct the transcript before it is made available for public use. Discuss potentially sensitive information with the narrator who gave it to you, confer with your committee and with other professional advisers about its historic value, then decide if and how you'll restrict such information. Many guides and manuals offer examples of how to restrict interviews. On the other hand, do not become so over-concerned with legal questions that you "lock up" your collection and avoid public presentation of some historically sensitive issues. It certainly would be a waste of effort if others could not enjoy the fruits of your labors and learn from some of the hard lessons of the past.

3. Legal concerns are not the only reasons that some oral history collections go unused. Some project directors and researchers view the project results as "theirs" and hold onto the collection in hopes of writing the definitive history of their community. Sometimes a project committee may lose steam and decide not to fulfill the public programming portion of their project. It is vital, however, to keep all promises made to narrators and to the community at large. At the very least, give copies of the interviews and transcripts (if available) to the narrators. The collection or copies of it should be deposited at the local library or a regional archive. Efforts should be made to use the interview material in some sort of public presentation, even if it is a simple talk or PowerPoint demonstration. Other researchers should be encouraged to use and expand on the historical work your group has completed.

4. One final consideration is important: economic outcomes. If the project is one that generates any economic return, the project has the responsibility to advise the narrators of this and to negotiate any reasonable remuneration. A "reasonable remuneration" will always depend on particular situations, but project directors and advisory committees should anticipate any necessary arrangements.

Having described how to develop community oral history projects and how to avoid the common problems that they may generate, we now provide ten examples of successful projects that have been implemented in recent years. The samples represent a range of regions, cultures, and methods. In the 1992 issue of this pamphlet, we included six other project examples—the Homewood-Brushton neighborhood in Pittsburgh, the Mountain Drive artists' community of Santa Barbara, two Iron Range communities in Minnesota, the El Barrio Popular Education Program of the Center for Puerto Rican Studies in New York City, homesteading women of Idaho's Owyhee County, and the sugar plantation community of Koloa, Hawaii. Each project had different purposes and challenges. Since 1992, a host of community-based and institution-based oral history projects have developed around the country. These projects sought to ask new questions and involve communities more closely in their production. All produced high-quality results, and several were nominated for or were the recipient of the biennial Oral History Association Project Award.

The projects described herein reveal that while community oral history projects can present difficulties in sustaining volunteer enthusiasm and obtaining adequate funding, they create ample rewards. Some projects focused on a specific place, such as a neighborhood; others documented communities of people residing within a larger area or from an occupational group. A few of the projects were designed to develop or add to a community archives, others to promote education, still others to involve the community in an institution's work of historical interpretation. Project directors explain why they chose particular topics, how they formed advisory committees, how projects developed, how they obtained funding and in-kind support, how communities participated, and what final products they created from the interviews. These examples also present suggestions for successful collaboration and how to avoid common obstacles facing community projects.

Communities of Memory: Searching for a Sense of Place in Alaska

A multi-ethnic project in Alaska reveals how a well-planned and executed community project can generate multiple oral history projects and programs over time. In the mid-1990s, the Alaska Humanities Forum staff realized upon reviewing some twenty years of grant proposals that many applicants consistently decried a loss of community spirit and integration. Proposal applicants noted that increased television watching and sudden increases in population triggered by the state's oil boom were most often causes of this change in community interrelationships. The solution, many contended, lay in re-invigorating the tradition of face-to-face interaction, thereby educating newcomers about the relationship of Alaskan people to their land and resources while integrating them into the community so that their new narratives became part of the community's story.

Alaska Humanities Forum staff designed a four-year statewide program to strengthen communities through oral tradition and oral history in a series of public forums. They obtained grant funding from the National Endowment for the Humanities, Rockefeller Foundation, Nathan Cummings Foundation, American Express Foundation, and a number of Alaska banks, businesses, and foundations. The Forum solicited proposals and selected communities which offered an active volunteer steering committee able to carry out the project, a strong local coordinator who had broad local support, and participation by all ethnic groups represented in the community in the planning and execution of the project.

Nine communities, chosen to represent the different regions and cultures of the state, selected a steering committee that interpreted the broad theme "stories of place," established sub-themes, selected the storytellers to be featured, and determined which parts of the recorded gathering would be edited into a product for statewide distribution.

Following many months of planning, each community staged a public storytelling/oral history gathering that involved wide community participation. The project drew on the strong tradition of oral narrative within Alaska's Native cultures and encouraged communication across age, economic, geographic, and ethnic boundaries. Statewide project director Patricia Partnow noted that "reactions to the public gatherings were extremely positive." A visiting folklorist, oral historian, or anthropologist served as consultant and discussant at each community gathering, then later produced an essay describing both the community-building process and the content of the stories shared. Each event was audio taped and videotaped, and materials deposited in the University of Alaska Fairbanks Oral History Archive.

After each symposium, local steering committees decided how to communicate their community's story to the rest of the state. Committees led community-wide discussions about the medium to be used and in the process explored other issues such as: Who writes the community history? How are diverse voices represented? Which narratives should be foregrounded? Must a unified picture of the community be drawn? If the medium of writing is chosen, how can the magical sense of *communitas* engendered during live performances be communicated? How can that sense be extended and built upon to inform future community-wide efforts?

As with most community projects, the Alaska project met challenges in obtaining adequate funding to ensure the project's continuity and in engaging narrators to critically reflect on their stories. Partnow advises that the only alternative to finding ample resources upfront is an assurance of long-term volunteer involvement. Another challenge was designing a forum in which community members examined their stories critically and comparatively. The celebration aspect was present at all gatherings, but a synthesis or analysis of how stories relate to community was harder to engender.

The project design worked well in a state that still relies on oral communication as its primary form of interaction. The project met greatest success in those places with broad institutional support, community support in public meetings, and the involvement of scholars in both planning and discussion following the gatherings. Partnow advises that "the single most important factor for success in this project model" is a strong local coordinator who is well known in all parts of the community, has strong cross-cultural communications skills, and is willing to volunteer much time to oversee local project activities. "Follow-through," she states, "is essential, especially after the excitement of the public gatherings has waned." Almost as important is a steering committee of individuals willing to expend time and energy on the project. Volunteers spent thousands of hours gathering the stories, transcribing, planning and executing the gatherings, and producing the accompanying materials from the recordings.

In addition to the hundreds of hours of recorded narratives archived at the University of Alaska, radio spots, a television program, books, and a calendar with oral histories were produced from the stories and distributed to participating communities and state libraries. In 2003 the University of Alaska Press published Phyllis Morrow's edited book about the project, *Communities of Memory*. Two of the most valuable aspects of the project were that community members spoke with one another, particularly across ethnic boundaries, and in about half of the communities the project generated additional oral history activities.

One of the communities in northwest Alaska, Nome, will be featured in a project that will experiment with new ways to present oral history on the web. In 2006, Will Schneider, Curator of Oral History at University of Alaska Fairbanks, obtained a grant from the Alaska Humanities Forum to advance the technological delivery of some of the recorded sessions from Nome, by producing synchronized searching of the stories on a project website. Synchronized searching allows one to simultaneously search by transcript, key word, photo, or section of video. During the summer of 2007, Schneider and Nome participants selected stories to feature and worked with Dr. Bob Jansen of Australia in developing the software and materials for the website. In Alaska, where travel is expensive and difficult, the Internet has provided an important means of disseminating oral history and information about communities. Nome has already produced a two-volume book and a video of the earlier *Communities of Memory* sessions, so there was strong local interest in developing more accessible and technologically sophisticated means of sharing community stories about subjects as diverse as the opening of relations with the Russian Far East, the history of the Iditarod, and Eskimo traditional knowledge. Schneider notes that the oral histories from Nome are particularly valuable because of their multi-ethnic quality, and he hopes this project "will [help] prove the technology" and also "help to reinforce the stories by keeping them in the public eye."

Voices from the Agricultural Labor Camps of Litchfield Park, Arizona

For some years, the Litchfield Park Historical Society (LPHS) wanted to document the memories and experiences of former residents of the thirteen migrant labor camps in Litchfield Park of the West Valley community of Maricopa County, Arizona. Established by Goodyear Farms in 1916 through its subsidiary, Southwest Cotton Company, the last of the labor camps was demolished in 1986. Little evidence exists today of the camps, as development and master-planned residential communities now prevail in Litchfield Park.

Like the initiators of many oral history projects, LPHS members recognized that there were fewer and fewer community members from the *campos* that were still alive. Yet hundreds of Mexican American families had worked in the labor camps and had contributed in numerous ways to the economic development and social and cultural life of Maricopa County. Some historical society members knew it was rather urgent to collect and preserve their stories, as many of the camp residents were elderly, but they were uncertain about how to launch the project and how "to do" oral history. Jose Leyba, a West Valley educator who himself had grown up in the camps, knew Gloria H. Cuadraz, a professor and oral historian from Arizona State University, and invited her to meet the women interested in launching a project. The women and Cuadraz explored the idea of a partnership and became enthusiastic about developing a project to preserve the history, stories, and cultural memories of former Mexican American residents who worked and lived in the Goodyear Farms "camps" between 1916 and 1986.

This collaboration between university professor and motivated historical society made the project a success. Cuadraz credits the "very strong historical society" and its oral history sub-committee of Belen Soto Moreno (former camp resident), Sonja Hendrick, and Sara Homen as absolutely critical to the project. The three women assisted in the planning, scheduling, and organizing of the project. They established initial contact with former camp residents; they scheduled interviews, and at least two of them were present for all the interviews conducted for the study. Cuadraz notes that "It was the kind of partnership where I couldn't have done the project without them, and they couldn't have done it without me. In that spirit, we have each grown in respect for each other and enjoyed the collaboration and the products of our labor."

Cuadraz notes that the major obstacle was in simply getting started. It took a couple of years of meetings with members of the LPHS before she was in a position to apply for monies to support the project and to have the time to dedicate to the project.

Project personnel pieced together funding from a variety of sources to support the interviews and a planned film and public programs. In 2005 they obtained a grant from the Arizona Humanities Council ($6025) and a matching grant ($3000) from Arizona Public Service (APS) to begin oral history documentation. This resulted in eighteen videotaped interviews, the production of a film based on these oral histories, Voices from the Camps of Litchfield Park, and a Founder's Day Reunion of the camp families.

In March 2006 LPHS organized a Founder's Day event or Reunion of Camp Families to share the project findings and to recruit additional participants. Over five hundred people, representing multiple generations of families who had worked and lived in the camps, attended the event. Some traveled from other communities within Arizona, and some from as far away as New York, Rhode Island, and California. Organizers showed the film, *Voices from the Camps,* which was well received, and through the course of the day identified additional participants for the study. A small photo exhibit was featured, in addition to lunch, mariachis, and time for families and friends to reunite.

A second grant from the Arizona Humanities Council in 2006–07 ($6025) continued the collection of oral histories and supported the production of a larger photo exhibit, "Images from the Camps." The exhibit is scheduled for Hispanic Heritage Month from September 8 through November 1, 2007 at Fletcher Library at ASU's West Campus and is designed to travel to local schools and organizations following the initial showing.

As with other community oral history projects, the Litchfield Park project depended on hundreds of hours of volunteer labor and donated expertise. The LPHS oral history sub-committee dedicated countless hours to the project. The support provided by Arizona State University reveals the benefits of collaboration with larger institutions in community history projects. Cuadraz was able to obtain some internal university grants to fund the collection of about half the videotaped oral histories. She volunteered her time and stretched resources by allocating funds to pay for student research assistants, videographers, and transcribers. The university also provided in-kind physical space for equipment and the services of support staff, campus graphic designers, public relations personnel, and IT staff who helped with the production of the film. Cuadraz explains that by cultivating "an ethos of excitement and responsibility in your campus community about the importance of your oral history project, you'll be pleasantly surprised at how many people will step forward to help you with whatever aspect of the project you're trying to achieve."

In addition to the successful partnership between LPHS and ASU, Cuadraz and the LPHS volunteers believe the most important aspect of the project was the production of the film into DVD format, which allows families to also own a composite view of the stories documented about the camps, in addition to their individual copies of their respective interviews.

The forty videotaped oral interviews, with the formal consent of the narrators, will be deposited in the Chicana/o Research Collection, Department of Archives & Special Manuscripts, of ASU's Hayden Library, with copies to the Litchfield Park Historical Society. Project personnel are currently submitting a grant through the Access and Preservation Office of the National Endowment for the Humanities to create an oral history platform for this collection and other oral history collections currently in need of preservation.

Cuadraz reports that the community response to the project has been overwhelmingly positive and that narrators and their family members have been especially appreciative of the team effort to complete the project. The project was designated a "We the People" Initiative from the National Endowment for the Humanities and received the WESTMARC (Western Maricopa Coalition, an organization of West Valley business and organizations) "Best of the West" Cultural Awareness Award in 2006. For her own role in the project, Cuadraz notes that it "has enriched my life in so many ways . . . If I were to do it all over again, the only difference would be that I would seek this kind of partnership for a community study much earlier in my academic career!"

Oral history projects can sometimes foster new community relationships and help to reconcile a divisive past with the present. A graduate student and community groups in Claiborne County, Mississippi collaborated to create *No Easy Journey,* an oral history project that generated a permanent exhibit, community forum, book, and play designed to recall the turbulent times of the civil rights movement in their community.

In the 1960s, civil rights activists in this rural, primarily African American community in southwestern Mississippi led an effective voter registration effort combined with an economic boycott. Local merchants in Port Gibson, Mississippi, responded to the boycott by filing an unsuccessful lawsuit against the NAACP and black citizens. This led to a unanimous landmark decision by the U.S. Supreme Court in 1982, affirming the right to protest by economic boycott. As a result of the local civil rights movement, black and white residents witnessed significant social change. Black elected officials in Claiborne County, for example, now number as high as in any county in the nation.

In 1992 Emilye Crosby interviewed a wide range of local civil rights activists, their opponents, and other residents for her Indiana University dissertation project, "Common Courtesy: The Civil Rights Movement in Claiborne County." Mississippi Cultural Crossroads (MCC), a local community arts and education organization, and local oral historians, folklorists, and civil rights activists developed a project that built on Crosby's research. MCC provided resources, community connections, and oral history training. The organization had sponsored an earlier oral history project, *i ain't lying,* and housed another, on the Farm Security Administration's Tenant Purchase Program, which influenced Crosby's research. MCC and Crosby formed a community advisory committee, including civil rights activists and opponents, which helped develop and oversee the oral history project. It was "very much a community project," says Crosby, "made possible by the time, memories, insights, and help of countless people, many of them current and former Claiborne County residents."

The project committee shared oral history narratives with the public through a play, exhibit, and forum. North Carolina poet and playwright Nayo Watkins created the play, *What It Is, This Freedom?* based on the oral histories gathered from county residents. Watkins staged two public readings and later revised the play based on community feedback and recruited local residents to act in it. The play's debut in 1994 provided an opportunity for commemoration and reflection with an opening forum, "Time for a Change," and premier of the exhibit, *No Easy Journey,* which documented the struggles that transformed the way blacks and whites would live together in Claiborne County.

The exhibit was permanently installed in the William "Matt" Ross County Administration Building in Port Gibson. School children, local officials, residents, and visitors now rely on it and related materials as significant resources. Tapes and available notes and transcripts are deposited at Mississippi Cultural Crossroads. The collection is listed in *A Guide to Oral History Collections in Mississippi* and the *Civil Rights Oral History Bibliography* on the University of Southern Mississippi website http://www.usm.edu/crdp/html/interviews/p-info.shtml.

Organizers of the *No Easy Journey* project had to be resourceful and pieced together funding from various sources to support specific project components. Crosby obtained some research and fieldwork support from Indiana University and the Carter G. Woodson Institute at the University of Virginia but most of her interviewing was "unfunded." After she completed graduate school, she later obtained some support for follow-up interviews from her employer, SUNY Geneseo. The Claiborne County Board of Supervisors hired five high school students to help with transcription, and the University of Southern Mississippi transcribed some interviews. The National Endowment for the Arts, through an Expansion Arts Grant, paid the playwright and director of *What It Is, This Freedom?* The Mississippi Humanities Council and Entergy financed the exhibit, and the Claiborne County Board of Supervisors provided permanent space for its display. The Mississippi Arts Commission, Claiborne County Board of Supervisors, and the City of Port Gibson contributed to some of the operating costs for MCC, which provided equipment and space for the project, coordinated the development of the exhibit, planned the forum, and produced the play. Community volunteers, MCC director Patty Crosby, the Community Advisory Committee, and several MCC Board Members donated their time to the project.

Project organizers met more difficult challenges than finding adequate resources. Staff and volunteers encountered lingering racism and some white opposition to highlighting civil rights history. Some residents considered the era a negative period in the community's history, so were reluctant to discuss it and opposed the exhibit. Despite early opposition, says Crosby, the community took a step toward acknowledging this shared history without "exploding." Those who initially opposed the project now see it as a positive contribution. In general, African American residents were pleased with *No Easy Journey.* Growing numbers of whites are coming to terms with the project; some now bring visitors to see the first such exhibit in a small Mississippi town. In such controversial projects, Crosby recommends staying true to the evidence, taking the time to include local people, and allowing the project to grow in other directions as community members shape it.

The now over 140 interviews collected have received extensive attention and use. The project also stimulated other oral history interviewing and dramatic performances based on interviews. In 2001–2002, MCC sponsored the Claiborne County Oral History Project, collecting and logging 27 interviews, and a photo documentation day to copy vintage photographs supplied by local citizens. In 2004 MCC hosted Port Gibson's "first ever" conference, "Telling the People's Story," supported by the Mississippi Humanities Council, which brought in people from around the nation to explore the ways in which community oral histories can be made accessible through public programs. In 2005 Crosby returned to the community to deliver a public lecture and booksigning for her recently published, *A Little Taste of Freedom: The Black Freedom Struggle in Claiborne County, Mississippi,* based on the interviews. The book is available at MCC and all local libraries. The next year, MCC developed a program for high school students that taught them how to use local and oral history in examining civil rights history. Some of the students created History Day projects that relied on No Easy Journey interviews and other materials. MCC is seeking funding to transcribe and digitize all the interviews on its website http://www.msculturalcrossroads.org/.

Many researchers like Crosby might have conducted oral interviews and included them in their scholarly work without returning that work in accessible formats to the community. But because of the MCC involvement and community interest in developing a wide variety of public programs, the *No Easy Journey* project became "far more accessible to many people." Crosby notes that facilitating community participation is time-consuming and requires patience. "True community involvement," she notes, "cannot happen overnight and makes projects take longer." But "without collaboration, it's unlikely that MCC or I would have been able to develop the exhibition, play, and related public forums."

The Disability Rights and Independent Living Movement Project

The Disability Rights and Independent Living Movement Project is a powerful example of collaboration between a community and a university-based oral history office (the Regional Oral History Office, or ROHO, at the Bancroft Library, University of California Berkeley). In 1982, Susan O'Hara, then director of the Disabled Students Program, approached Willa Baum, then director of ROHO, with the idea of documenting Berkeley's strong disability rights movement. In her own oral history O'Hara later reflected, "I think having majored in European and American history in college and having taught it for thirteen years, I just had a sense of history. It was almost impossible for me to be around Berkeley in the seventies without sensing that there was something very important going on here." O'Hara, Baum and several disability activists secured modest funding from the Prytanean Society at UC Berkeley, and completed the first two interviews in 1984 and 1985.

In the early and mid-1990s activists from disability rights organizations such as the Center for Independent Living contacted the Bancroft Library to ask whether it would preserve their organizations' records. Their leaders were aging and their papers were stacked in basements and attics. "They saw a need and we saw the historical value of these records. They were willing to collaborate," said project director Ann Lage of the library. "It's the greatest team effort I have ever been involved with."

The Bancroft Library successfully applied to the National Institute on Disability and Rehabilitation Research, an agency within the U. S. Department of Education for funding for the project. Oral history interviews began in earnest in 1996. Susan O'Hara and Disability Rights Education and Defense Fund co-founder Mary Lou Breslin helped to form an advisory board and drew in people from the community to be interviewers. The advisory board worked together to select the narrators and helped to build trust between ROHO and the community. "Without that trust-building the project would not have been successful," explained Lage. "It would not have worked for the university to just knock on people's doors."

The collaborative nature of the project—among the disability community, academic advisors, oral historians, and archivists—strengthened it in every respect. Understanding that oral history is most often successfully carried out by people who combine a compelling personal interest in the project with an ability to bring a historical perspective to their task, ROHO turned to disability rights activists themselves to staff the project's team of interviewers. All project interviewers had personal experience with disability. A majority had significant disabilities; several had participated in or observed the historical events to be documented and knew many of the key players and organizations. Interviewers were trained in oral history methodology and paid for their work. As the interviewing proceeded, the coordinators sought feedback from the project team members and advisors, as well as at public presentations given at conferences of the Society for Disability Studies, the Organization of American Historians, and the Oral History Association.

The project team selected narrators who fit at least one of several criteria: they were a founder or recognized leader of one of the key institutions, made a unique contribution to the movement, developed into a particularly keen observer and articulate reporter, or became a sustainer of the movement who provided a unique perspective. The project coordinators attempted to choose narrators who had a range of disabilities and to interview non-disabled persons who contributed significantly to events or institutions.

All of the project interviewers met monthly as a group to plan and evaluate interviews and review progress. Interviewers prepared a preliminary outline before each interview session based on background research in relevant papers, consultation with the narrator's colleagues, and mutual planning with the narrator. In-depth tape-recorded interview sessions were from one to two hours in length; narrators required from one to fifteen sessions to complete their oral histories, depending on the length and complexity of their involvement in the movement.

The project was completed in two phases. The first phase, completed in 2000, documented the movement during its formative years in Berkeley. During this phase interviewers recorded forty-six oral histories with Berkeley leaders, many of whom have also been figures on the national scene, and the Library collected personal papers of narrators and others in the disability community and archival records of key disability organizations. After Phase I was completed the oral histories were shared in a day-long symposium, "Intersections of Civil Rights and Social Movements: Putting Disability in Its Place," which took place at UC Berkeley on November 3, 2000. This symposium brought together more than 300 scholars, activists, students, and community members to discuss the disability movement within the larger context of a broad range of American social movements. Transcripts from that symposium are available online at the Disability Rights and Independent Living Movement website.

Phase II of the Project (2000–2004) expanded the oral history research and the collection of archival material to document the growth of the movement nationwide. The project again focused on those leaders whose activism began in the 1960s and 1970s. The original project team, primarily based in Berkeley, all contributed to the design of the project and assisted in developing interview protocols.

A closely related Artists with Disabilities oral history project conducted by ROHO oral historian Esther Ehrlich included interviews with five pioneering performance artists and dancers with disabilities. Funded in part by a grant from the National Endowment for the Arts, the interviews in this collection explored the lives and works of these seminal artists in dance and performance art.

During their review of the verbatim transcripts, narrators were asked to clarify imprecise passages and to provide additional information when needed, but to preserve the transcript as much as possible as a faithful record of the interview session. The final stage of processing added subject headings, a table of contents, and an index (for the print versions). ROHO offered narrators the opportunity to seal sensitive portions of their transcripts or omit them from the Internet versions.

According to ROHO's project statement: "The oral histories give voice to many key players in the disability community. They include activists who applied lessons from the civil rights movement to disability rights, lobbyists and attorneys who developed disability rights law and policy, pioneering parents of disabled children, architectural designers and community advocates focused on accessibility, professors who helped establish disability studies as a discipline, artists with disabilities, and more."

More than 100 oral histories have been completed, with more planned for the future. In addition, a rich collection of personal papers and the records of key disability organizations accompanies the oral histories in the Bancroft Library, comprising an in-depth research resource for the study of a contemporary social movement which has transformed the social, cultural, and legal landscape of the United States. ROHO's Disability Rights and Independent Living Movement website http://bancroft.berkeley.edu/ collections/ drilm/index.html links to more than 8,000 pages of the project's interview transcriptions in the California Digital Library—fully searchable by keyword through the Online Archive of California. The oral histories are also available at the Bancroft Library.

Documenting Washington, D.C.'s Gay, Lesbian, Bisexual, and Transgendered History

Some community oral history projects are motivated by a lack of information about their community to create new institutions or associations to document their history. Frustrated by trying to identify sources of information on gay, lesbian, bisexual, and transgendered history in Washington, D.C., Mark Meinke placed a notice in the *Washington Blade* inviting GLBT community members to start a documentary history project. Five people showed up the next Saturday, November 4, 2000, for a meeting at the CyberStop Cafe on 17th Street NW and founded the Rainbow History Project. The group's mission is to collect, preserve, and promote an active knowledge of the history, arts, and culture relevant to sexually diverse communities in metropolitan Washington, D.C.

At its first meeting, the Rainbow History Project decided to make its priority the collecting of community oral histories. Project organizers began interviewing a wide variety of people from ethnic, religious, sexual, gender, political, economic, racial, social, and other backgrounds about what it has meant to be gay, lesbian, bisexual, transgendered, or queer in Washington since the 1950s. Mark Meinke reports that, "Rainbow History works very hard to ensure that its collection reflects the demographics of its community." The project has had some difficulty in getting bisexuals and the transgendered to share their stories. Meinke notes that project participants work to ensure that the collection is not just about the "important people" in the community. "Everyone has a story to tell and we work to get everyone to tell their story."

The Rainbow History Project's activities are planned democratically and include executive and advisory boards. An executive board of directors, elected for two-year terms, plans and organizes the projects. All dues-paying members are eligible to vote and to be elected to the board. An advisory board of twenty-five community members, archivists, and historians (gay and straight) helps maintain the Project's professional integrity and provides crucial resources for documenting the history of the community. The Project is funded by membership fees ($25 membership), individual contributions, grants from a number of funding agencies, dedicated fundraisers, and contributions for specific projects.

The Project is especially conscious of the needs of narrators and the potentially sensitive nature of the subject matter. Interviewers allow narrators a great deal of latitude in controlling the direction, detail, and intimacy of the stories she or he tells. When the interviewer asks the narrator to further expand on areas of the story, in all cases the narrator has the last word on whether she or he wishes to elaborate.

Issues of privacy are particularly significant in doing GLBT oral history. Each narrator of a life story signs a release form giving Rainbow History full rights to the recording and its contents. These rights can be, and often are, limited in writing on the release by the narrator. However, the Project takes further steps to protect narrators. It never releases a recording or a transcript, even if it has the right to do so, without first contacting the narrator for his or her permission. Many times Rainbow History puts the narrator in touch with the person who has requested the interview so that they can discuss how it will be used and what the purpose of the research might be.

Just six years after the initial six volunteers organized it, the Rainbow History Project has developed an impressive oral history collection and receives growing interest from all across the country. But as with other community projects, the group faces funding challenges. According to project chair John Olinger, "We operate on a budget of about six to seven thousand dollars. When we have volunteers available to help, we transcribe the tapes." One way to meet this challenge "is to expand our membership and engage younger members of the community." The labor-intensive nature of sharing the project findings also increases costs. Olinger explains, "The tapes are accessible to interested researchers after we inform the narrator, who has the final say over access to his or her narrative."

In addition to assisting researchers interested in the materials, the project has used the oral narratives in a series of gay D.C. tour brochures. Rainbow History has also drawn on the narratives to produce special features, such as anniversaries of important events or places, which are posted on the website: http://www.rainbow history.org/. Rainbow History walking tours and presentations to community groups also incorporate material from the oral histories.

Publishing Oral History to Engender Community in New Hill, North Carolina

Sometimes a community oral history project is triggered by a crisis and sustained by a dedicated volunteer. The rural, racially mixed community of New Hill, North Carolina, had undergone several major developments that threatened its autonomy and traditional way of life. A nuclear power plant, manmade reservoir, and a major interstate highway had already changed the rural landscape, and a new sewage plant was proposed to be located in the community's center near its historic district.

New Hill residents responded to this latest threat by forming a community association, which met alternately at the First Baptist Church of New Hill, attended by African American residents, and the New Hill Baptist Church, attended by white residents. The New Hill Community Association members hired an environmental attorney and conducted fundraising activities to pay legal fees. One of the fundraising projects was a book of stories from long-time area residents. Judy Tysmans, a relative newcomer to the community who worked at the University of North Carolina at Chapel Hill (UNC-CH), conducted the oral interviews and compiled historical and recent photographs to produce the publication.

Tysmans had previously conducted a family oral history project, but called on Beth Millwood of the UNC-CH Southern Oral History Program to provide professional expertise to the New Hill group. In September 2005 a team from the Southern Oral History Program came to a community meeting and suggested ways to organize the project, as well as recommended funding sources and sample interview release forms.

Judy Tysmans conducted and transcribed most of the interviews, but New Hill community members helped in other ways. They provided the names and phone numbers of people who were good storytellers, and made available their own historical photographs, maps, and recipes they remembered for inclusion in the book. The New Hill Community Association president, Paul Barth, promoted the book at meetings, suggested an inexpensive printing shop and picked up book copies from the printers to keep them available. One community member transcribed an interview, and another offered to digitize the cassette tapes and back them up on her hard drive. Another donated a case of cassettes to use in recording interviews. Tysman's husband, Dirk, a computer programmer, provided technical support with scanning and suggestions concerning the publication's layout. Katie Nordt, a North Carolina

State University Graphic Arts major, used the text and pictures from the book for her senior project, adding photos of her own and designing the book. Remaining grant funds from the New Hill Community Association will fund printing a "coffee table" version of the book and make it available to local businesses.

Some obstacles hindered the timely completion of the New Hill Oral History Project. Interviewer Judy Tysmans ended up transcribing most of the interviews, which was extremely time-consuming. She recommends that other community oral history projects submit a grant proposal to hire a transcriber. As an "outsider" to the African American community, Tysmans also found it difficult to garner interviews from its members. Another major problem came from the fact that New Hill was a very small community where people knew their neighbors well over a long period of time. Some people preferred submitting two-page essays giving minimum information about their lives and experiences, rather than run the risk of offending community members (some of whom had been dead for over fifty years) in a recorded interview.

Tysmans found that oral history research led to intellectual rewards as well as contributing to the community. She took a graduate seminar in Remembering with Professor Della Pollock in Communication Studies at UNC, which provided an opportunity to discuss with others how and why people's memories are "adjusted" in various ways over time. "The sharing with others in the field about our mutual struggles," reported Tysmans, "provided validation and encouragement for me in my work."

The very positive attitude in the community about having the book to read and share with family members was the major incentive that kept Tysmans working on the project. *The Oral Histories of New Hill, NC* has sold about one hundred copies, and more will be printed. The oral history project and book helped build the community's cohesiveness and preserve its original identity. It likewise achieved its original goal to raise funds for the New Hill Community Association and its work to prevent further environmental degradation of the community.

Museum & Community Collaboration: the Stonington Fishing Oral History Project

Sometimes the realization that a declining community should be documented prompts an oral history project. For over 200 years, Stonington Borough in Connecticut has been tied to fishing. But the twenty-five boat Stonington fishing fleet, the last commercial fishing fleet in Connecticut, faces an uncertain future. "Fishing here—and throughout the world—is in real trouble," observes Fred Calabretta, Curator of Collections and Oral Historian at Mystic Seaport, The Museum of America and the Sea. To document the disappearing fisheries and the Stonington fleet's history, the museum initiated a series of oral history and photographic projects.

In 1993, with an initial $6,000 grant from Community Foundation of Southeastern Connecticut, the Stonington Fishing Oral History Project began collecting interviews with fishermen and their families. The Woman's Seamen's Friend Society of Connecticut provided a $2,000 grant for videotaping the fleet.

The interviews revealed that the fortunes of this fishing community fluctuated with the vagaries of the economy and environmental change throughout the twentieth century. Although vessels, gear, and technology were among the subjects emphasized in the interviews, the chief focus of the project was the community's residents, including the large percentage of fishermen and their families of Portuguese descent. By documenting the lives of Stonington people, the oral history project revealed changing generational perspectives, the importance of family and tradition, the influence of advancing technologies, the interaction of ethnic groups and their cultures, the state of the fishing industry past and present, and the changing face of an occupational community engaged in an ancient endeavor.

The Community Foundation provided an additional $12,500 to continue the project and support the development of an exhibit, which was first presented during the annual Blessing of the Fleet in Stonington in 1995. Project staff installed the exhibit, comprised of forty enlarged prints and interview quotations from the oral history project, in Mystic Seaport's Mallory Building. At the request of the fishing community, the exhibit returned to Stonington's annual Blessing of the Fleet through 2005—a run of ten years. Because of budget limitations at the museum and the need to refresh the exhibit materials, staff declined the invitation to continue the presentation in 2006.

The story of the Stonington Fishing Fleet is represented in a major, long-term exhibit the museum opened in 1999 entitled *Voyages: Stories of America and the Sea*. The fisheries section of the exhibit features a profile of one of the Stonington fishermen interviewed for the project. It includes photos, fishing gear, and clothing the fisherman donated for the museum's permanent collections and an edited video program based on materials gathered for the project.

In 2004 the museum published a book entitled *Fishing Out of Stonington: Voices of the Fishing Families of Stonington,* which project director Calabretta edited. Excerpts of oral history interviews accompanied by a selection of the Project's photos form the core of the book. It is noteworthy that a regional charitable foundation, the Community Foundation of Southeastern Connecticut, provided some funding for the book, after providing prior funding for the original project. This demonstrates how a successful community project culminated in a long-term relationship with a foundation that was willing to provide financial support for a decade.

The Stonington Fishing Oral History Collection is part of Mystic Seaport's broader collection of maritime holdings exploring coastal community life in New England. The project has collected 35 interview recordings, over 800 pages of transcripts, over 1,400 photographs, and the one-hour videotape. The collection has been thoroughly catalogued and cross referenced for rapid access to selected speakers, eras, and topics and is now housed in the G. W. Blunt White Library, the research library of Mystic Seaport Museum that specializes in American maritime history. The project materials (interview recordings, transcripts, and photos) have been used extensively by researchers, including students in the museum's Williams-Mystic program, an undergraduate maritime studies program. The project description has been made available online at http://www.mysticseaport.org/library/collections/stonfishaccess.cfm and researchers can access catalog records for the interviews by clicking on the links for collections and sound recordings.

Although project director Calabretta regrets that lack of time and funding has limited the scope of the Stonington Project, the interviews and exhibit established an important, new, and ongoing relationship with the Stonington fishing community. The effort required to make contacts and establish community relationships has created a more positive connection between Mystic Seaport and the fishermen and families of Stonington Borough. Connecticut Public Television also produced a program, *Connecticut and the Sea,* based on the contacts produced by the project.

The Stonington project met some difficulties based on the nature of the work it documented. Since fishermen work outdoors, interviewing and photography depended on the cooperation of the weather. In addition, the fishermen are often gone for long periods of time. When they come home, they want to be with their families rather than standing on the dock talking to an interviewer. Calabretta notes that he dealt with these issues by trying to accommodate the community members' schedules and remaining flexible. "As a standard policy," says Calabretta, "consideration for the narrator is an obligation. The payoff is great, not just because it's the right thing to do, but also because such consideration contributes to the success of the project." The project's success, which was only achieved through a good relationship with the community, states Calabretta, was the preservation of the memories of Stonington fishing families' experiences, lifestyles, and traditions.

Cushman Motor Works Centennial Oral History Project, Lincoln, Nebraska

This project documented workers' perspectives of the evolution of Cushman, Inc., (known at the time of the project as Cushman, A Textron Company), a manufacturer of widely known brands of motors, scooters, golf carts, and other small utility vehicles. The firm, which was founded in Lincoln, Nebraska, in 1901, began preparations for commemorating its centennial in 2001. Sharon Burcham, former president of Local 5-0907 of the Paper Allied Chemical Energy Workers Union, knew that the stories of former company employees, many of whom had spent decades with this prominent local business, should be recorded for the celebration. She became the driving force behind the Cushman oral history project. The scope of the project covered perspectives on factory life from the World War II years as part of the defense industry, to the most recent years of corporate change related to shifts in the international economy. The project also created a particular opportunity to document the changing role of women and minorities in this blue-collar manufacturing plant.

Burcham worked in collaboration with the Cushman Community Involvement Team, a group of managers and employees, and contacted staff familiar with oral history at the Nebraska State Historical Society. The local union obtained a grant from the Nebraska Humanities Council (NHC), which funded critical interviewer training by professional oral historians Barbara W. Sommer and Mary Kay Quinlan, as well as supplies and interview transcription. The Nebraska State Historical Society loaned recording equipment to the interviewers. Thirteen company retirees and current employees volunteered to conduct the oral history project and completed sixty-four interviews.

A second NHC grant and funds from the local union supported publication of a book entitled *The People Who Made It Work: A Centennial Oral History of the Cushman Motor Works*. Historians Quinlan and Sommer wrote the text, basing it on all the interviews, photographs, and other historical materials collected during the project. Cushman's parent company, Textron, provided in-kind support for the book's layout, design and publication.

The key public presentation occurred at the company's centennial celebration in June 2001, which hundreds of current and former Cushman employees attended. Quinlan and Sommer spoke about the project and distributed copies of the book. Photos and a timeline developed as part of the original oral history project were used as the basis of exhibit panels displayed at the plant's anniversary celebration. Sommer and Quinlan have also presented a slide show/lecture about the project through the Nebraska Humanities Council speakers' bureau and the Nebraska State Historical Society's Brown Bag luncheon series. The project donated copies of the book to the Lincoln Public Library, and it deposited the oral history interviews in the Nebraska State Historical Society.

Timing can be key to carrying out a successful community oral history project, as former Cushman employees discovered. Ironically, within months of the project's completion and Cushman's centennial celebration, the parent company closed the Lincoln plant. If the oral history project had not commenced two years earlier, it would have been virtually impossible to complete once the plant closed and its workers scattered.

Like most community history projects, lack of time and transcribed interviews created some obstacles to completing the public presentation portion of the project. The book project had a tight deadline in order to be completed by the anniversary celebration, and the interviews had not been transcribed by the time the book needed to be written. The existing collection of historical materials and photographs had never been sorted or catalogued in any manner. The book's authors, Sommer and Quinlan, worked diligently to organize the materials and were eventually able to use excerpts from all sixty-four interviews in the final publication.

Sommer and Quinlan credited the high-quality interviews produced and the overall success of the Cushman Oral History Project to advance planning spearheaded by local union leader Sharon Burcham. The planning process provided adequate training for volunteer interviewers, as well as helped project directors anticipate expenses that in-kind efforts could not cover. This strong planning component allowed the project staff to create a support system that kept the project focused and moving in the right direction. The community of Cushman workers helped create a lasting legacy that documented their role in the company, rather than another corporate history devoid of the human stories about life on the plant floor.

The Missouri Historical Society (MHS) turned to the oral history method to document people's perceptions of how and why neighborhoods change, what remains the same, and how and why people create community. The resulting project, Through the Eyes of a Child, provides a model for community involvement in producing oral history and in using interviews in multiple formats for public audiences.

Through the Eyes of a Child: Neighborhood Oral History in St. Louis

MHS oral historian Jacqueline K. Dace designed the project to focus on four St. Louis neighborhoods within which the African American population equaled or exceeded seventy percent of the total population between 1940 and 1980, to provide a representative cross-section of African American community life. With limited funding provided from 1995 to 1998, Dace reached out to neighborhood members of Kinloch, the Ville, and Carr Square in Missouri, and the south end of East St. Louis in Illinois to participate.

Community involvement was key in planning and implementing the project. In 1996, after a series of community-based focus group meetings, MHS brought together five groups of representatives from St. Louis's African American community and solicited feedback on the type of history project they wanted MHS to undertake. They responded that they wanted the work to show the daily lives and struggles of residents from an African American perspective, to provide both historical and contemporary insights, to involve community members, and to appeal to young people.

Through community input, the committee decided to focus the project on the institutions and resources that shaped children's lives between the 1940s and 1980s. MHS staff responded with an initial project proposal for a neighborhood-based oral history project. An advisory board comprised of the diverse class, educational, and generational perspectives of St. Louis's African American community approved the proposal and continued to offer guidance and assistance through the duration of the project.

The project, based on the premise of the African proverb "It Takes a Village to Raise a Child," sought to determine how that village manifests itself. Beginning with a biographical overview of the narrator's life, interviewers asked about everything from the importance of community centers, schools and churches, to neighborhood friendships and distant relatives, to perceptions of how particular boundaries for each neighborhood shaped the narrator's childhood development.

Prior to conducting interviews, staff conducted comprehensive neighborhood research. Using census data to characterize the neighborhoods from 1940–1980, researchers examined differences in census tracts and developed broad descriptions of the overall population, education levels, school population, total home ownership and income levels. Project director Dace notes that balancing statistical, library, and historical research with oral histories is important in documenting the ways in which people create community. She advises when organizing a community oral history project to, "Find something in the research that you really enjoy and have fun while getting the work done."

Securing funding was a persistent challenge for the project. In March 1998, Through the Eyes of a Child received additional support from a local philanthropic organization, the Whitaker Foundation. MHS provided a part-time research assistant for eighteen months as well as equipment and supplies. A research fellow and a student intern from Eastern University worked on the project in the summer of 1998.

Flexibility was necessary in dealing with delays caused by lack of staffing, scheduling difficulties with MHS and community members, and a necessary change of outcomes. The initial project goal was to develop an exhibition based on the community oral histories, but this had to be changed due to a major construction extension to the MHS museum. Community members helped MHS staff re-frame the outcomes of the project. Instead of an exhibit, project designers produced a documentary video to distribute to community groups and libraries throughout the region. In February 2000 the documentary premiered at the Hollywood Black Film Festival where it was honored with an award for best documentary. As part of the Whitaker Foundation grant, project staff created curriculum materials, which they distributed with the video to approximately 600 junior high schools in the metropolitan area. The documentary continues to be used in conjunction with MHS programming to initiate similar community oral history projects by residents of other St. Louis neighborhoods.

Another major component of the project included the development of a play, *Through the Eyes of a Child: Coming Home,* written by Historyonics Theatre Company director Patton Chiles. With the script crafted from the verbatim words spoken in the oral history interviews, the play was initially performed in front of a wildly enthusiastic audience consisting of former and current residents of selected neighborhoods and those who had taken part in the project.

In addition to the video and play, St. Louis residents have been introduced to Through the Eyes of a Child through other formats. Not only was the undertaking described on local radio and television programs, but the half-hour documentary video was broadcast over the local public television stations. With additional funding provided by a gift from local philanthropist Mrs. Myron Glassberg, the exhibit, *Through the Eyes of a Child: Growing Up Black in St. Louis, 1940–1980,* based on the oral history research opened at the MHS in March 2003 and ran through February 2004. Since then, students and scholars have used in their research the original tape recordings and transcripts archived at the MHS Library and Research Center. Dace has also presented this research to numerous local community organizations, university classes, and fellow historians at national conferences. Based on the successful input and assistance of community members, MHS staff have sought to initiate similar projects with residents of other neighborhoods.

In 2002 Dace developed a companion project, In the Voice of a Child, to fulfill the community advisory committee's request that the project reach young people. Through the Rockefeller Foundation Partnerships Affirming Community Transformation two-year grant, Dace worked with five middle schools in the St. Louis area to introduce the oral history curriculum unit to the classroom environment. In the Voice of a Child allowed students not only an opportunity to listen to their elders but also to speak for them, through a project that employed their choice of one of several artistic media (a play, radio program, book or magazine, video production, or exhibition). A team of artists and professionals facilitated by St. Louis Public Schools Department of Community Education mentored the students, who presented their final projects to a larger audience, first at the MHS, then in an additional public venue.

Successful efforts at creating committed community volunteers, finding appropriate funding sources, situating the project within a local historical society, and celebrating the oral histories with the original communities allowed this project to create multiple products over many years. Project director Dace reports that community response to Through the Eyes of a Child has been "phenomenal," because the project illuminates day-to-day life in St. Louis' African American communities. Dace reminds project organizers that compromise is essential in collaborative work. "If you plan on partnering with a community organization," she says, "understand that their criteria and deadlines may not be the same as yours. Understand their commitments and make sure they coincide with your mission. Rigid dates will only frustrate you and cause conflict within the project. Do not relinquish authority, but at the same time be open to adjustments enough to allow others to claim ownership."

Uncovering the Hidden History of Seattle's Chinese Americans

Oral history is at the core of most projects at the Wing Luke Asian Museum of Seattle, Washington. The museum once focused on its collection of valuable Asian artifacts, but then changed its direction to reflect the lives of Asians who made their way to the U. S. rather than the lives they left behind. It began to collect ordinary artifacts from people's experiences and started gathering first-person oral history information from the city's Asian American communities to complement the material objects.

Museum director Ron Chew recognized the need to document Seattle's diverse Asian American communities and spearheaded the eight-year Chinese Oral History Project, which focused on individual lives and the evolution of the Chinese American community from 1860 through the 1960s. Chew initially gathered twelve volunteers to interview approximately one hundred Chinese elders in Seattle. The project became a true community effort through volunteer participation in all stages of project development.

When he initiated the project in the early 1990s, Chew was advised to bring in expert interviewers from outside the community who would have the emotional detachment to ask sensitive questions. But he knew that "insider" status was critical, since Chinese elders would not open up to strangers, especially those who needed interpreters. Language barriers, a history of illegal status, and the impacts of racial discrimination would have impeded an honest exchange of information. To overcome these difficulties and to gain access to elders, Chew trained members of the Chinese American community in interviewing techniques. By building trust and encouraging active community participation, Chew and the volunteers broke the barriers of suspicion and gained the cooperation of most elders.

The Chinese Oral History Project collected hidden histories and also brought closer together different generations. Many Chinese immigrants had not spoken of their past, even to their children, for fear of deportation. Grandchildren interviewed grandparents, children talked with parents, and narrators often revealed stories that had been buried for generations. Seattle's Chinese Americans told immigrant tales of repression and quiet resistance, recalling the exodus to the United States in search of wealth, the gold mines of California, and the impact of exclusionary legislation that existed until 1944. The Chinese Exclusion Act of 1882 prohibited immigration and naturalization and prompted some Chinese to create false pasts, with the false stories becoming familiar family history. Some elderly Chinese, still fearful of deportation, were reluctant to tell their actual stories. But since interviewers clearly communicated the project's objective to create a more honest portrayal of the Chinese immigrant experience, many became willing to share their experiences.

Volunteers became critical to the success of the project. Over 150 volunteers participated in the project at various stages, with substantial donations of time to identify potential narrators, conduct research, develop interview questions, interview, collect photographs, and translate and transcribe interviews. An initial grant of $6,500 from the King County Cultural Resources Division funded the first part of the project to help cover the costs involved in photography, transcription, and translation. Wing Luke Museum staff donated much of their time.

According to project director Chew, it was important to build outcomes into an oral history project so that staff, volunteers, and participants understood and worked toward concrete goals.

In addition to an extensive oral archive, now housed in the collections department of the Wing Luke Asian Museum, the oral history interviews spawned a book, *Reflections of Seattle's Chinese Americans: The First 100 Years,* edited by Chew. It is already in a second edition with additional oral histories gathered since 1994. An exhibit of the same name traveled throughout the region.

Delving into the origins of the Chinese American community in Seattle, researchers continue to use the oral history interview materials at Wing Luke. The Chinese Oral History Project was one of the springboards for other oral history projects at the museum and in the area, such as Densho, the Seattle-based digital archive and learning center dedicated to preserve the testimonies of Japanese Americans who were unjustly incarcerated during World War II. The Wing Luke oral history project has provided material for exhibitions, such as *If Tired Hands Could Talk: Stories of Asian Garment Workers in Seattle,* documentary films such as *Finding Home in Chinatown: The Kong Yick Buildings,* and other research projects, including genealogical investigation by local families.

Recognizing that a project will usually take longer than anticipated, lining up committed volunteers, and having some individual or individuals to coordinate the project, will insure success, advises Chew. The Chinese Oral History Project revitalized an interest in the history of Seattle's Asian Americans and generated pride and support in the Chinese American community. Because it involved both civic leaders and ordinary people, it forged cooperation and trust that empowered the community to record its neglected history. It also created for others rich resources that will increase understanding of Chinese American history.

Books

There are numerous guides to oral history, and the following examples can instruct in or lead you to more sources about community projects, interview techniques, recording equipment, preservation, interpretation, and public programs.

Allen, Barbara and Lynwood Montell. *From Memory to History: Using Oral Sources in Local Historical Research.* Jackson, MS: University of Mississippi Press, 1991.

Charlton, Thomas L., Lois E. Myers and Rebecca Sharpless, eds. *Handbook of Oral History.* New York: AltaMira Press, 2006.

Dunaway, David K. and Willa K. Baum, eds. *Oral History: An Interdisciplinary Anthology.* Walnut Creek, CA: AltaMira, 1996.

Frisch, Michael. *A Shared Authority: Essays on the Craft and Meaning of Oral and Public History.* Albany, NY: State University of New York Press, 1990.

Grele, Ronald J., ed. *Envelopes of Sound: The Art of Oral History.* New York: Praeger, 1991.

Ives, Edward D. *The Tape-Recorded Interview: A Manual for Fieldworkers in Folklore and Oral History.* Second Edition. Knoxville: University of Tennessee Press, 1995.

_____. *An Oral Historian's Work.* [Video] Blue Hills Falls, ME: Northeast Historic Film, 1988.

Perks, Robert and Alistair Thompson, eds. *The Oral History Reader.* Second Edition. London: Routledge, 2006.

Portelli, Alessandro. *The Battle of Valle Giulia: Oral History and the Art of Dialogue.* Madison, WI: University of Wisconsin Press, 1997.

Ritchie, Donald. *Doing Oral History: A Practical Guide.* Second Edition. New York: Oxford University Press, 2003.

Schneider, William. *Project Jukebox: Where Oral History and Technology Come Together.* Anchorage: University of Alaska Press, 1992.

Sommer, Barbara W. and Mary Kay Quinlan. *The Oral History Manual.* Lanham, MD: AltaMira Press, 2003.

Stielow, Frederick J. *The Management of Oral History Sound Archives.* Westport, CT: Greenwood Press, 1986.

Thompson, Paul. *The Voice of the Past: Oral History.* Third Edition. New York: Oxford University Press, 2000.

Yow, Valerie Raleigh. *Recording Oral History: A Practical Guide for Social Scientists.* Second Edition. Lanham, MD: AltaMira Press, 2005.

SUGGESTED RESOURCES

The Oral History Association (OHA) offers many resources. Its website http://www.dickinson.edu/oha links to dozens of projects and programs across the country with online digital recordings, guides to oral history collections, curriculum materials, and more. OHA organizes an annual meeting, publishes *The Oral History Review*, a newsletter and the following pamphlets:

Oral History Association Pamphlets and Other Resources

Barnickel, Linda. *Oral History for the Family Historian: A Basic Guide* (2006).

Mercier, Laurie and Madeline Buckendorf. *Using Oral History in Community History Projects.* Second Edition. (2007)

Neuenschwander, John A. *Oral History and the Law.* Third Edition. (2002).

Wood, Linda P. *Oral History Projects in Your Classroom* (2001).

Oral History Evaluation Guidelines (2003) Available as a pamphlet, or for free at http://www.dickinson.edu.

For more information about the Oral History Association, or to order copies of the pamphlets listed above, contact the Oral History Association, Dickinson College, P.O. Box 1773, Carlisle, PA 17013, (717) 245-1036; e-mail: oha@dickinson.edu.

In addition to the resources available through the Oral History Association, organizations such as the American Association for State and Local History, National Council on Public History, and the Organization of American Historians offer technical leaflets, journals, and guides to community and oral history research.

There are hundreds of valuable websites featuring community oral history, too numerous to mention here and whose web addresses are likely to change. The following are suggestions to get you started in surveying the rich resources, guides, and model projects available online.

Other Websites

Baylor University Institute for Oral History. "Oral History Workshop on the Web." http://www.baylor.edu/oral_history/index.php?id=23560

H-OralHist http://www.h-net.org/~oralhist/. Discussion listserv includes a searchable archive on topics ranging from equipment to ethics.

Mercier, Laurie, ed. "Using and Interpreting Oral History Interviews." *Columbia River Basin Ethnic History Archive* (2003). http://www.vancouver.wsu.edu/crbeha/tutorials/int_oh.htm

Portelli, Alessandro, and Charles Hardy III, "I Can Almost See the Lights of Home: A Field Trip to Harlan County, Kentucky," *Journal for MultiMedia History,* vol. 2 (1992). http://www.albany.edu/jmmh/vol2no1/lights.html

Shopes, Linda. "Making Sense of Oral History." *History Matters: The U.S. Survey Course on the Web,* February 2002. http://historymatters.gmu.edu/mse/oral/

Vermont Folklife Center. Includes an excellent *Audio Field Recording Guide* written by Andy Kolovos that covers latest technological issues in oral history recording equipment. http://www.vermontfolklifecenter.org/res_audioequip.htm

www.ingramcontent.com/pod-product-compliance
Lightning Source LLC
Chambersburg PA
CBHW081157090426
42736CB00017B/3362

* 9 7 8 0 9 8 4 5 9 4 7 1 9 *